A MAN'S RIGHT TO
HAPPINESS

A MAN'S RIGHT TO
HAPPINESS

by Laissez Faire Contributors

aissez Faire Books

An Essential Resource for Enlightened Minds Since 1972

ISBN: 978-1-6212910-4-6 (print)
ISBN: 978-1-6212910-5-3 (ebook)

18 17 16 15 14   2 3 4 5 6 7

Published by Laissez Faire Books, 808 St. Paul Street, Baltimore, Maryland
www.lfb.org

Cover and Layout Design: Andre Cawley

CONTENTS

INTRODUCTION

In many ways, our way of life is under attack.

It's the little things, mostly. We don't even notice the small and seemingly insignificant events that slowly erode our lifestyle like a poorly tended beachfront.

Day to day, you can't see any difference. But left unattended over a number of seasons, the beach disappears, leaving beautiful beachfront properties exposed to the relentless surf.

Take inflation, for example. Each year, the Fed's target inflation rate is set at 2%. This means if Ben Bernanke (or soon, Janet Yellen) gets his way, everything we buy is 2% more expensive year after year.

Doesn't sound like much, Over time, though, that tidy nest egg you build up won't go as far as you once thought.

As I said, it's often the little things that add up.

But then there are big events that occasionally shake our understanding of the world. The events surrounding Sept. 11 come to mind. The housing boom and resulting bust is another. The ongoing revelations being made by Edward Snowden is a more current example.

Big or small, these events are influenced, or even instigated, by our government. And they have an impact on all of our lives.

Yet we still dream. We strive for a more enjoyable and meaningful existence. We still work towards a better life for ourselves and our children.

Searching for new ways to improve our lives beyond the wants of D.C. and Wall Street… this is the goal of Laissez Faire Books. This book, *A Man's Right to Happiness*, is just the beginning of the discussion.

The topics covered in the following pages are some of the most pressing issues at the moment. But the future will bring more problems.

So we'll continue the conversation in the *Laissez Faire Letter.*

In the *Laissez Faire Letter,* we are assembling a group of experts who will help you find better ways to prepare for retirement, ways around destructive legislation, and actionable things you can do to improve your life… today.

In short, we're searching for better ways to live life on our own… without the "helping hand" of government. So we can live healthier, wealthier and longer lives and give a better future to our children than the one we inherited.

— Doug Hill
Director, *Laissez Faire Club*

1 THE OBAMACARE ANTIDOTE
6 Ways to Get the Best Health Care of Your Life and Save up to $2,000 per Year

"One of the main problems with health care reform is ideological, rather than economic. Rather than focus on improving the quality and price of goods and service across the marketplace to the benefit of rich and poor alike, there has been a great deal of emphasis on **equalizing** the market position of the rich and poor alike."

— Kevin D. Williamson

"The End Is Near and It's Going to Be Awesome"

Would you dress up in your finest suit or pull out your nicest dress to go to the **emergency room**? That's what one expert suggests might be necessary as the country gets ready to implement the largest reforms in our health care industry.

According to Richard Maybury, author of *Early Warning Report*, "The problem with medical care is that the industry has been made political since the days of FDR. As a result, in order to get good care these days, you have to game the system."

By this Maybury means you have to be truly informed and understand more about the socialistic chaos within the complex bureaucratic health care system than the care providers do. Doctors and administrators within hospitals will likely be guided more than ever by government-mandated rules than your actual care. Add to this mix an additional 20–30 million newly insured individuals and you can envision pure chaos in hospital emergency rooms as well as doctor offices.

If by happenstance you require emergency triage, Maybury recommends that you transform your image as much as possible to that of a health care provider. He means that doctors and nurses are social beings that will gravitate more quickly and attentively to those with whom they identify the most. Therefore, if you dress intelligently, sound highly educated, act very polite and courteous, and perhaps carry a book with you, health care providers may feel more inclined to pay more attention to you and provide better care.

This is the kind of mindset you'll need in the new Obamacare America.

Now before you panic, take comfort knowing I've written this report to show you how to jump off the track and avoid the Obamacare train wreck careening toward you.

Driven by my personal struggles with my health care business and my inability to obtain health insurance due to a pre-existing condition (I'll explain more about it later on), I have researched and identified six entrepreneurial and innovative solutions just for you.

I'm confident that combining any of these solutions with other supplemental insurance coverage will save you an immense amount of time, money, and frustration, while at the same time let you obtain access to world-class health care.

Here's a quick glimpse on what you can expect in this report.

1. How Obamacare Will Affect You
2. Medical Tourism
3. Private Medical Lab Testing Service
4. MediBid — Online Marketplace
5. Surgery Center of Oklahoma — New Model
6. Shop & Negotiate for a Lower Price
7. Concierge Care — Direct Primary Care
8. Take Responsibility
9. Recommendations

We're going to cover a lot of information in the next few pages. But it will all be worth it. When the president's law starts collapsing under its own weight, you'll be glad you took the time to protect yourself.

So with that in mind, let's begin.

HOW OBAMACARE WILL AFFECT YOU

As you read this report, it's important that you understand Obamacare does not change our health care system. We will still have the same hospitals, procedures, protocols, safety standards, and advanced equipment and instrumentation. What has changed are the tax codes and insurance rules across the nation as well as incentives. These changes will impact everyone in the form of higher prices and rationing.

Our goal in this report is to arm you with the information necessary to prepare to slowly "opt out" of this system and take back control of your health care.

For the purposes of this report, we will assume that you fall under one of the following health insurance categories and then address how you can survive the adverse effects under each scenario:

1. You are currently **uninsured or underinsured.**
2. You purchased **private insurance** in the individual market.
3. You are insured through your **employer.**
4. As a **baby boomer**, you receive, or will soon receive, **Medicare**.

Let's go through each scenario separately.

1. **You are currently uninsured or underinsured.**
   - You will now be required to purchase health insurance through a government-operated online exchange and cannot be denied coverage
   - Failure to purchase insurance will result in a penalty (tax) from the Internal Revenue Service. The maximum tax amounts are as follows: $285 in 2014, $975 in 2015, and $2,085 in 2016
   - The premium cost of most policies in the exchange will be expensive. All insurance companies will be forced to cover all applicants regardless of age or health conditions, including individuals with chronic illnesses
   - This may be good for middle-aged and older individuals, but not for younger citizens, who are generally healthier and require much less care. They will now be hit with much higher premiums to support the sick and elderly.

2. You purchase private insurance in the individual market.

- As promised by the Obama administration, "If you like your insurance, you will be able to keep it." However, expect to pay much higher premiums. As mentioned above, all insurance companies will be forced to cover all applicants regardless of age or health conditions, including individuals with chronic illnesses

- As a small-business owner with 50 or more employees, you will be required to provide health insurance to those who work over 30 hours per week or you will be fined $2,000 for each. (Note: As of July 2013, the government delayed implementing the employer mandate. Individuals will still be required to acquire insurance if they aren't covered.)

Did You Know... Under The New Obamacare Mandate

- Under Obamacare, we can expect stratospheric private health insurance premiums, deteriorating levels of care, lost jobs, and a recessionary economy. President Barack Obama and uber-wealthy (former) Speaker Nancy Pelosi will, obviously, never have to experience the adverse effects of their health care reform.

- Doctor shortages — The Association of American Medical Colleges estimates that by 2015 the country will need 60,000 more doctors than it is expected to have by then. (from Obamacare Survival Guide, pg 181.)

- Nearly one-quarter of all seniors rely on Medicare Advantage, the private health care option in Medicare. However, Obamacare makes such deep cuts to that program that half of those covered will no longer be able to keep the coverage they have.

- Tens of millions will lose their employer provided insurance because of the perverse incentives under the program. Even the establishment CBO admits that at least 7 million, and as many as 20 million, will lose their employer coverage.

- Under the Obamacare law, the employer mandate does not require employers to cover the family dependents of their workers. So the trend towards losing that coverage is already beginning.

- "Section 3000 A" of the Affordable Care Act, awards bonus points to hospitals that spend the least per senior patient.

---

3. **You are insured through your employer.**
   - Most likely, you have already seen increases in your premiums and deductibles.
   - You will face the potential risk of your employer dropping your insurance coverage as the cost outweighs the benefits
   - Companies with 50 or more employees will be required to provide health insurance to all full-time workers, which is 30 hours or more per week under the ACA, or be fined $2,000 for each employee not covered
   - Hourly workers might get their hours cut in order to make them part-time employees. Employers would then not have to provide them insurance.

4. **You are a baby boomer covered under Medicare.**
   - Seniors are the hardest-hit group under the new health care law
   - The act established a presidential commission called the Independent Payment Advisory Board (IPAB), which has been directed to cut Medicare spending in the future because its decisions will automatically take effect
   - The law cut Medicare by $716 billion in order to partially fund $1.9 trillion in new entitlement spending over the next 10 years
   - Section 3000 A of the Affordable Care Act awards bonus points to hospitals that spend the least per senior.

GET WORLD-CLASS SURGICAL CARE AT 80% OFF THROUGH MEDICAL TOURISM

Medical tourism is when you travel out of your local area to receive medical treatment. The term "medical tourism" is actually a misnomer, coined as such by the national news media to describe the phenomenon of Americans traveling to tropical destinations for cosmetic and dental procedures.

If you really think about it, people have been traveling great distances for thousands of years in search of pain relief and longevity. In the past century, people from every corner of the planet have traveled to the U.S. to receive the most advanced treatments from renowned hospitals like

Johns Hopkins, the Mayo Clinic, Mass General, and MD Anderson.

But in case you missed it, a new trend in medical tourism emerged in North America about 10 years ago. Uninsured and underinsured Americans began traveling to exotic destinations for surgical procedures. Motivated by the high cost of care in the U.S. along with the technological advancement of hospitals in emerging economies, American patients save literally thousands of dollars on elective procedures. These range from hip/knee replacements and heart bypass surgeries to spinal fusions and dental implants.

You may even be surprised to learn that an entire medical tourism industry has arisen in the U.S. to cater to patients seeking to escape from our excessively expensive health care system.

A quick search in your Internet browser for "medical travel" or "medical tourism" will quickly yield pages upon pages of results for specialized travel agencies. Known as facilitators, these highly advanced hospitals in foreign countries directly target medical tourists. And as an entrepreneur and owner of one such service, **MedRetreat**, I have firsthand experience when it comes to this business.

To date, the most popular destinations for medical tourists are Costa Rica, Brazil, India, Malaysia, Mexico, Singapore, South Korea, and Thailand. Most elective surgical procedures in these countries are 50–80% less expensive than in the U.S.

Consider this example. A hip replacement without insurance in the U.S. can cost anywhere from $45,000–70,000, depending upon the hospital and location. However, depending on the country you travel to, the same hip replacement typically ranges from $10,000–18,000. So you can see that even when you factor in all the travel- and boarding-related expenses, you can easily save $20,000–40,000. That's huge!

Of course, the obvious question is, "But is it safe?" With the right information, medical tourism is very safe, for a few very important reasons:

1. Medical tourism is not new. Citizens from Great Britain, Canada, and other countries with socialized health care systems have been traveling for medical procedures for decades in order to escape long wait periods and rationed care in their own countries.

2. Large hospitals actively market and promote their services to foreigners as a way to benchmark their global brand success domestically and increase healthy profit margins from cash-paying medical tourists.

3. Foreign hospitals that cater to international patients actively pursue accreditation from globally known organizations like the Joint Commission on Hospital Accreditation (JCAHO), a U.S. safety accreditation organization.

4. Globalization. Elite hospitals around the world have caught up in terms of facilities, equipment, safety procedures, standards, and protocols. Many well-known foreign hospitals partner with Johns Hopkins and Harvard Medical to share best practices and cross-training exercises.

5. Lastly, Adam Smith's "invisible hand" incentives principal. The last thing any of these elite hospitals that promote medical tourism want is a dead American patient in their hospital. Such a scenario would likely be international headline news the next day, resulting in substantial brand damage.

Information is your key to success when considering surgical procedures in foreign countries. There are essentially two ways to pursue health care abroad: direct or through a medical travel facilitator.

Direct simply means that you do all the research online and contact the foreign hospital on your own. Typically, you will find a patient inquiry form on the hospital's Internet homepage. You will be asked to provide basic contact information and list the procedure that you are seeking. Once submitted, you can expect an email reply within 24–48 hours. However, it may even be as long as a week, in some instances.

Once you have scheduled all treatment logistics with the doctor and hospital, you will then need to coordinate all travel-related details. In some cases, the hospital is prepared to assist you with most of these details.

A more efficient method for booking a surgical retreat in a foreign country is to work through a U.S.-based medical tourism facilitation agency. These agencies have established a global network of hospital partners and can assist you will all the details of your entire trip. These include planning, pricing, hospital stay, communications, flights, transportation to and from the airport, and hotel stay for recuperation. Many of these agencies even have destination program managers who will assist you and act as a representative and friend during your stay.

One big advantage to using an agency is their relationships with their hospital partners. Should any problem arise during your stay, your agency has a great deal of leverage in resolving disputes, since they will have developed a strong rapport with key high-level managers and doctors.

If you would like to learn more about medical tourism or **MedRetreat**, you can contact at the following:

Web Address: www.MedRetreat.com
Toll Free: 877-876-3373
Email: customerservice@medretreat.com

SAVE HUNDREDS OF DOLLARS USING PRIVATE MEDICAL LAB TESTING SERVICE

There's a reason why this next solution is so important to me. You see, for years as an entrepreneur I was fortunate enough to have comprehensive health insurance through my wife's large employer.

Then, in early 2011, my health coverage luck ran out when my wife's engineering position was terminated as a result of a private equity leveraged buyout.

After a short stint on COBRA, I researched the private insurance market for my family. Unfortunately, I quickly learned that no private insurer would cover me because I had been diagnosed with Crohn's disease, an incurable inflamed bowel.

Now, for the first time in my adult life, I am uninsured.

Now, a simple thyroid-stimulating hormone (THS) level test within the established medical network could cost me about $500.

But what I learned next was more valuable than gold. Approaching my health care as I would approach buying a new TV or refrigerator, I was able to save close to $350 on my blood work, *even without insurance*.

By going directly through an online **private lab testing service**, the actual cost was $148. That's real savings!

Here's the story…

One morning, I called my doctor's office to get my thyroid prescription refilled. The receptionist said I would need to see my doctor so she could provide me with the lab work request form for the required TSH panel. My condition requires me to regularly measure my thyroid hormone level.

Since I had no insurance coverage, I asked the receptionist about the costs involved. She said the first visit would be $98, the lab work would be around $400, and the follow-up visit would be another $98 to interpret the lab report and fill the prescription.

The grand total? $596 for a "simple" refill of my medication.

I sat stunned in silence.

Then I started thinking. I knew from my own health care business experience, there had to be a less expensive way. All I had to do was find it.

Within an hour, I succeeded. You should get a pen and paper and write this down.

Private MD Labs provides confidential laboratory testing and personal medical information direct to the public. Their model empowers you to take charge of your own health and assists you in the prevention and early detection of disease.

Even better, there's no physician's referral needed. You request the test you need and pay directly. No insurance company is involved to drive up unnecessary administrative costs.

I quickly found the test I needed on their website and clicked on it. To my amazement, the total cost for the test and lab work was $49! Just 12% of the $400 fee I would have paid directly to my doctor _for the same exact work_.

Two hours later, I received an email containing my lab work request form with a doctor signature contracted through Private MD Labs. Along with the form, they sent a list of the labs near me where I could go to have my blood drawn.

The following day, I drove to a local lab, where I waited in the lobby for about 20 minutes. I had my results 24 hours later. The old, expensive way usually took three–five business days to get my lab results.

When I explained to my doctor how I did this, her jaw dropped. She had never heard of this service before.

As for me, I was thrilled. I received faster service and had to pay only 25% of the traditional costs. If I had simply accepted the existing, bloated system, I would have been out $596.

An additional benefit of using one of these online private lab testing service is that once you create a user account that is password-protected, all your panel lab reports are stored for future use. This really comes in handy as you track your personal health data. You will be able to see if your medication is working or not before your next doctor visit.

Here are some reputable online private lab testing service you can try.

1. Walk-In Labs: http://www.walkinlab.com
2. Personal Labs: http://www.personalabs.com
3. Private MD Labs: http://www.privatemdlabs.com

I chose Private MD Labs for my blood work because their website was straightforward and easy to navigate. After using them several times now, I can vouch for their great customer service and timely responses too.

USE COMPETITION TO SAVE MONEY USING THIS ONLINE MARKETPLACE

The "eBay" or "Travelocity" of medical care?

MediBid is an online marketplace for health care services and is based on a model of transparency, competition, and market principles. Patients in need of any kind of medical procedure can simply visit MediBid's website, create a profile, create a request, and then collect competitive price bids from physicians from around the globe. Once all the bids are collected, the patient can review and select their top choice.

The key stipulations with MediBid is that the patient will most likely be required to:

1. Travel to the destination where the doctor performs their procedures and
2. Pay cash in full, upfront.

On their website, MediBid claims they can save users up to 80% savings through their bidding service.

According to Dr. John Goodman, health policy expert and president of the National Center for Policy Analysis, "Patients typically save one-third of the average cost, which is certainly significant savings on big-ticket procedures like joint replacements or spinal procedures."

KNOW BEFORE YOU GO: SURGICAL PRICING "A LA CARTE"

The Surgery Center of Oklahoma is a doctor-owned, cash-pay-only hospital that was established in 1997 to provide the highest quality of care at the most affordable price. Today, the total cost of their surgical procedures (which are all listed online) is one-sixth the cost of the same procedures performed elsewhere.

Complex Bilateral Sinus Procedure

Local nearby hospital $33,505, not including the surgeon's or anesthesiologist's fees

Surgery Center of OK $5,885, all inclusive

If you think I'm making these numbers up, you can check them out yourself: http://www.surgerycenterok.com/pricing/

Let me give you some background to this story.

Frustrated by the gross inefficiencies and ever-rising cost in health care, Dr. Keith Smith, an anesthesiologist at St. Anthony Hospital in Oklahoma, made the decision to actually do something about it. He, along with partner, Dr. Steve Lantier, tendered their resignations in 1997 and founded the Surgery Center of Oklahoma.

Dr. Smith, a self-described libertarian thinker wanted to escape the diabolical and parasitic three-way marriage between Big Government, big hospitals, and big insurance companies who were gaming the health care system to enrich themselves at the expense of the patients.

From the outset, Dr. Smith guided his financial operating model with the patient at the core of his strategic vision and the end goal of providing the highest quality of care at the lowest cost.

To accomplish this goal, Dr. Smith had to first abolish administration overhead. All staff members of the Surgery Center are directly involved with patient care in one way or another. Bean counters need not apply.

The next dramatic step was to eradicate the relationship with big government and big insurance. By not accepting Medicare, Medicaid, and insurance, the Surgery Center was no longer entangled in manipulation and price gouging of the patient. Since all patients pay for their care with cash, the Surgery Center has the ability to negotiate a fair and reasonable price that is completely transparent and win-win for all parties.

The Surgery Center really made big waves in 2009 when Dr. Smith created a website where he listed all procedure prices online for all to see. For the first time, any patient could actually go to a website and see how much their medical procedure would cost. This action led to an significant inflow of medical tourists from Canada.

The consumer-driven model that Dr. Smith created has made a significant impact on the quality and cost of care. A ReasonTV report on the Surgery Center describes a patient in need of a complex bilateral sinus procedure. A nearby hospital quoted the patient's bill at $33,505, not including the surgeon's or anesthesiologist's fees. However, the all-inclusive price at the Surgery Center was $5,885.

The Surgery Center offers a diverse array of medical procedures at approximately one-sixth the cost elsewhere. That includes orthopedics, ear/nose/throat, general surgery, urology, ophthalmology, foot and ankle, and reconstructive plastics.

For a complete listing of procedures and prices at the Surgery Center, please visit: http://www.surgerycenterok.com

9500 N. Broadway Ext.
Oklahoma City, OK 73114
Tel: (405) 475-0678

Many doctors and health care specialists believe that the Surgery Center of Oklahoma model will become more common with the implementation of Obamacare. However, one substantial impediment will be the certificate of need (CON) laws. This requires all medical facilities to obtain permission from a planning board of local hospital administrators before opening.

This regulation is essentially a gift to all established hospitals. It keeps any potential competitors at bay. Oklahoma happens to be one of the few states that does not have the CON law.

Additionally, a new provision in Obamacare effectively prohibits doctors from starting their own hospitals or expanding hospitals that they already own.

If you happen to have a high deductible through your insurance policy or have no insurance, the Surgery Center of Oklahoma is an excellent option for obtaining the highest quality of care at a very affordable price. The only stipulations are that you will have to pay upfront in cash and you will have to travel to Oklahoma.

On a final note, Dr. Keith Smith is an entrepreneurial health care visionary and champion of liberty and free markets. You can follow his health care blog at: http://www.theconservativepundit.net/

SHOP & NEGOTIATE FOR A LOWER PRICE

You wouldn't want to negotiate with a car salesman for that new Audi that you really want without doing your homework on the pricing, dealer incentives, and invoicing. The same rule applies to medical procedures when you are paying out of pocket and it works. According to Todd Roscoe, a former executive at the hospital chain Tenet Healthcare, "a 40% discount off the inflated list price is the norm for cash-paying customers."

One of the biggest problems in modern-day health care is the lack of knowledge when it comes to pricing. If you are not insured and or have a very high deductible and want to see how much it would cost for an operation for a torn meniscus at your local hospital, you are most likely out of luck. They have no idea.

The reason for this is straightforward. The vast majority of health care services in the U.S. (about 80% of them) are paid by a third party. So for most of us, our medical bills are paid by our health insurance, or some government-run programs like Medicaid or Medicare.

This arrangement completely cuts out you, the end customer. And because you aren't paying for it directly, the costs don't matter.

But what if you have to actually pay for your next surgical procedure? Whether uninsured or underinsured, you can negotiate the price with your surgeon. In fact many new business have sprung up in the past few years (which we will share with you below) to help patients navigate this tricky process.

The secret here is that when you are a cash-paying customer, doctors and hospitals are able to offer price discounts. The key is that you must be armed with the right information.

IMPORTANT PRICE CONSIDERATIONS AT THE BEGINNING OF YOUR SEARCH:

1. **Will your surgical procedure be inpatient or outpatient?**

   Inpatient means that you will be admitted to the hospital postop for a period of time for recovery. Outpatient means that you will be released from the hospital postop. The average cost for staying overnight in a hospital room is approximately $1,700. Obviously, you want to limit your hospital stay as much as possible.

2. **Can your surgery be performed in an outpatient surgery center instead of a hospital?**

Many medical specialties, like orthopedics and cardiology have set up outpatient surgery centers apart from hospitals. These centers can be quite a bit less expensive. Their business models are much different than large tertiary care hospitals, where a significant portion of their cost structure comes from diagnostics. Additionally, these centers have much more leeway in price negotiations.

3. **Do you know all the health care providers that will be involved in your treatment?**

Before your scheduled treatment date, find out all the providers who will be involved in your case. These include anesthesiologists, pathologists, radiologists and pharmacists. All if these care providers may bill separately from the hospital and the surgeon. You want to find out what their fees will be. Be sure to inform them that you will be paying cash and negotiate for the best price.

4. **Do you know the average price that insurance companies are paying for different procedures — the group negotiated rate?**

Large health insurance companies negotiate the prices that they will pay for most procedures of their policyholders. This negotiated price is much lower than the price that an uninsured patient will pay for the exact same procedure. Healthcarebluebook.com is a new online service that can help you determine what the fair prices of medical procedures in your area are.

5. **The hospital bill?**

Most hospital bills are nearly impossible comprehend. They are incredibly long and riddled with medical terminology that is difficult, if not impossible, for the average layperson to decipher. Hospitals could certainly simplify their bills by streamlining and translating medical terms so that we could all understand them, but why would that want to do that? It would tip the negotiating power away from the hospital billing staff and to you.

Fortunately, there are many new companies that will negotiate the bill on your behalf. These consultants are hospital billing experts and know how to spot the negotiable hidden discounts. They also know the discounted rates that insurance companies are paying for medical procedures. Most hospital billing experts claim that it is not uncommon to obtain a 40–50% reduction from their original price.

Here are a few hospital billing negotiation services you can use the next time you're in a jam:

Healthcare Blue Book
Medical Cost Advocate
Hospital Bill Review
My Medical Negotiator

Negotiating Bargaining Chips:

1. First, you should understand that you have nothing to lose by negotiating your hospital charges. Quite possibly, you could save up to 50%.

2. As soon as you learn that you must enter the hospital for treatment, make sure to tell your doctor and hospital administration that you will be paying cash upfront (if possible) and want their lowest price.

3. Do your homework and learn exactly what is involved in your procedure:

   a. What is involved and how long will the procedure take?

   b. What technology will be used? Newer equipment is more expensive.

   c. Inpatient or outpatient? Request outpatient if at all possible.

   d. Can you pre-prescribe or bring your own medication?

Obtain price quotes from medical tourism agencies and/or the Surgery Center of Oklahoma and then present them to your local hospital for competitive bid.

RESEARCH DOCTORS ONLINE AND BOOK YOUR OWN APPOINTMENTS

In addition to the traditional shopping methods for doctors in your local area or using one of the resources highlighted in this report such as a medical tourism facilitation, MediBid, or the Surgery Center of Oklahoma, there are several Web-based platforms for researching doctors and scheduling appointments. These websites provide detailed information about doctors, including their contact information, backgrounds, expertise, patient opinions, and even bedside manners. Such sites will prove immensely beneficial when you are a cash-paying health care consumer and not being directed by your insurance provider:

1. Healthgrades — Founded in 1998, Healthgrades is the leading independent health care ratings company for doctors and hospitals. Their online decision support tools enable patients to research and compare doctors across a range of professional and personal attributes and book appointments online. Healthgrades does charge a fee for viewing detailed information about the doctors.

2. FindaDoc is an online search tool for locating and researching doctors, both domestic and international. FindaDoc employs a unique proprietary rating system that helps patients rate doctors on their training, expertise, and patient opinions. FindaDoc is currently free for patient use.

3. ZocDoc is an online health care provider research and appointment booking service with thousands of specialists throughout the U.S. You simply type in your ZIP code and indicate what type of doctor you are seeking. Within seconds, multiple doctors in your local area are listed, along with pertinent information about their training and experience. Once you click on your doctor of interest, their appointment schedule appears on your screen, so that you can type in your desired date and time. ZocDoc is currently free for patient use.

"BEST EVER" ACCESS TO YOUR DOCTOR WITH MEDICAL CONCIERGE SERVICE

Remember the days when doctors would show up at your home for if you needed it? Well, today, innovative doctors are bringing that idea to the 21st century.

A recent entrepreneurial development in health care delivery is the formation of medical concierge services, or "boutique medicine." Physicians that offer concierge service continue seeing their existing patients enrolled in private insurance, but offer premium concierge services to patients that are willing to pay an additional retainer fee.

The average fee ranges between $1,000–4,000 per year, though some have been found for as little as $50 per month. In exchange, the patients typically receive the additional services:

• Cellphone number provided to call physician at any time
• 24/7 access
• Same-day appointments
• Longer appointment times
• Home visits.

The trend in concierge medicine has grown as physicians have become increasingly frustrated by bureaucratic red tape, administrative paperwork, and loss of control from both private insurance and government regulations and want to provide the highest level of service to their patients.

Unfortunately, the Affordable Care Act/Obamacare didn't solve any of the existing problems facing physicians in caring for their patients. In fact, the new law exacerbates the problems by adding approximately 20 million new patients to the U.S. health care system.

In the past year, private physicians have been turning to the concierge model at a very rapid pace. According to a Marketwatch report, there were approximately 4,400 doctors providing concierge service in 2012, a 25% increase from 2011.

During my last doctor's visit in May of this year, I asked my physician about concierge service. She informed me that she is already in the process of establishing one for her practice and would be sending out letters to all her patients in the coming months.

If you have the financial means, enrolling in such a medical concierge service is an excellent option. As concierge services evolve over time, doctors will be positioned nicely to add new value-added features. These will enhance overall communications and monitoring of your health care status.

As an example, you can simply obtain lab work directly through private lab testing services, such as Private MD labs, and then send the results directly to your doctor for review. Your doctor can then call you directly to discuss your lab results and then call in prescriptions for you without having to schedule appointments and driving to and from office visits. This will save a great deal of time and frustration.

Other technologies coming online include smartphone apps that monitor a whole host of different anatomical readings. These include your heart rate, blood pressure, temperature, etc. (I have listed several of this aps below.)

Also, multiple companies are currently manufacturing devices known as "labs on a chip." These will be mass-marketed in a few years' time, which may make lab visits obsolete. A small sample of blood and saliva tests will be encrypted and uploaded into a "cloud service." Your doctor can then access if from anywhere in the world.

Such technological advances combined with direct 24/7 access to your doctor through a concierge service will radically change the delivery of health care. It will tear down the walls between you and your doctor forever.

TAKE RESPONSIBILITY OF YOUR OWN HEALTH AND AVOID UNNEEDED TRIPS TO THE DOCTOR

With the enactment of the Affordable Care Act, health care reform is a reality for us all. This disruptive bureaucratic behemoth is already causing immense chaos and confusion.

We are bombarded by daily news reports that the Department of Health and Human Services (DHHS) key directives of the individual state insurance exchanges are running behind schedule. Even President Obama has been emphasizing publicly that the new reforms will encounter hiccups, or "bumps in the road."

Going forward, my best advice is to avoid the health care system as much as possible. You must adapt and change your view of our medical system and how you use it.

Now is not the time to maintain the status quo in the management of your own personal health care. Your immediate goal must be to prepare as much as possible to stay out of the system. Take inventory of your current health status and then develop strategies and goals for how you can best achieve your optimum health so as to avoid our health care system.

The good news is that there is an overflowing abundance of information and technological tools at your disposal for learning and tracking all of our vital health data. With the aid of social media and smartphone apps, we are able to connect to a global network of the latest health care and medical information 24/7. This network enables us to share, motivate, inspire, and learn how to nourish our bodies and minds as never before.

Some Healthy Suggestions for Taking Control:

1. You already know the basics: healthy meals with plenty of fruits and vegetables; daily exercise; a good night's sleep; healthy relationships; minimal stress; and, of course, not smoking and limiting your alcohol consumption.

2. Just take out your smartphone and search the app store and you will quickly find a number of health tools enabling you to track, share, plan, set goals, etc. Here are some highly rated ones for you to try:

    > Workout Trainer
    > RunKeeper
    > MapMyRun
    > Endomondo Sports Tracker
    > FitnessBuilder
    > Gorilla Workout

3. Before January 2014, talk to your family physician about the impending changes that will come with the Affordable Care Act. What are his or her plans? Are they planning on offering a concierge or premium service, as highlighted above, that you can join? Is he or she retiring? What's their recommendation?

4. Set up and store all your personal health data electronically. These include: your doctor name and contact information, blood test results, doctor visits, weight, allergies, blood type and pressure, medications, past surgeries, mental health, substance abuse and addictions.

    Here are some of the more popular electronic personal health record apps for your computer, tablet, and smartphone.

    > Microsoft HealthVault
    > My Life Record App
    > My Medical
    > Capzule

5. Purchase an electronic activity tracker today and start using it. The most popular brands to date are Fitbit, Nike Fuel, and Jawbone Up. These small devices can easily be attached to your clothing or worn on your wrist. Wear it at all times. They track all your activity, including steps taken, stairs climbed, calories burned, miles walked, and even sleep. These are guaranteed to motivate you to live a more active life.

    I purchased the Fitbit for $99. It syncs wirelessly with my computer and smartphone. After using it for a couple of days, I became totally addicted to looking at it throughout the day to see if I am close to reaching my activity goals.

6. Purchase a juicer and begin juicing at least two times per day. You would be amazed how great a smoothie tastes with a combination of kale, spinach, blueberries, strawberries, bananas, almond milk, and vanilla yogurt. My personal favorite it the Nutribullet, which I purchased at Target for $99.00 over a year ago and use twice a day.

MY HEALTH CARE RECOMMENDATION

As we enter this period of massive health care disruption brought about by the Obamacare legislation, there will be multiple opportunities to obtain world-class health care at a very affordable price. The key is having the right frame of mind about health care and staying informed about all the new entrepreneurial solutions that are sprouting up to meet the needs of this ever-evolving market.

The goal of this report is to provide you with some of the best alternatives available today in the health care marketplace. Each solution is chosen to save you time, money, and frustration. Some of these alternatives may not be right for you at this time or fit your specific needs. However, I believe that mixing and matching some of these alternatives with your insurance policy will provide you with the best quality in health care at an affordable price and in a timely fashion.

So here's the plan I intend to employ.

1. **Change your mindset** and start taking responsibility for your health. A significant proportion of your health is determined by your behavior, which for the most part is determined by your habits. Healthy habits boil down to discipline, nutrition, and exercise. As we all know, this is easier said than done. However, there are so many new tools and applications for tracking all your health-related goals and stats that really go a long way in motivating you to staying the course.

2. **Tweak Your Insurance Plan:** When Obamacare is fully implemented, I would suggest converting your current insurance coverage to a plan with the lowest premium possible while complying to the Affordable Care Act in order to avoid the penalty. The lower your premium is, the higher your copays and deductibles will be. But bear in mind that you will be able to apply these savings to the options highlighted in this report.

   Normally, I would suggest a catastrophic plan. They are designed to provide emergency safety nets only. Unfortunately, the Affordable Care Act deems catastrophic plans as "unqualified." Meaning if you buy a catastrophic plan, you'll still be subject to the tax outlined in the introduction of this report.

   But you should be able to find coverage plan with lower premiums than you are paying now.

   If you are uninsured or underinsured due to a pre-existing condition and are forced to purchase insurance through government-mandated state insurance exchange, I would suggest that you select the "Bronze Plan," which is the least expensive plan. This is the one that I intend to enroll in. For more information about these plans, you can view the exchange at: https://www.healthcare.gov/what-is-the-health-insurance-marketplace/

3. **Medical Concierge:** Then I suggest that you enroll in a medical concierge service, which will likely cost you anywhere between $1,000–4,000 per year. The amount of money that you will be saving on your lower monthly insurance premiums should cover most of the concierge expense.

    Through a concierge model, you will have constant access to your doctor, longer appointment times, and all-around better service. You won't be waiting for weeks or months to see your doctor, like most others.

4. **Private Medical Lab Testing:** Now, since you will be facing a high insurance deductible, you can turn to one or several of our alternatives the we have outlined here in this report, which are more compatible to cash-paying patients. To begin with, you can now obtain any required lab work from a private medical lab testing service like Private MD Labs.

5. **Shop & Compare Procedure Price:** For many surgical procedures that you may require, such as a hernia repair, torn meniscus repair, angioplasty, hysterectomy, vasectomy, and/or deviated septum, will most likely not meet your high deductible. In this instance, you will be required to shop, meaning that you will have several options to consider for obtaining the highest quality at the best price.

    The best way to begin is to identify how much your procedure will cost at your nearest hospital. Be sure to inform all doctors and administrators that you will be paying cash upfront and want their best price. Next you can visit Healthcare Blue Book, an online resource listed in the Shop & Compare section of this report, to identify the fair price that you should expect to pay for your particular procedure.

6. **Negotiate Procedure Price:** Once armed with the pricing information, you are ready to begin comparing your other options in the following order:
   • Negotiate with your local hospital for their lowest price
   • Check out pricing at Surgery Center of Oklahoma.
   • Contact a medical tourism facilitation agency like MedRetreat
   • Go back to you nearest hospital and show them price quotes from Surgery Center of Oklahoma and medical tourism facilitation agency.

7. **Comprehensive Physical Exam:** One last suggestion that you should consider pertaining to preventive care is that of comprehensive physical exams. These should be conducted every five-10 years after the age of 40.

   These type of exams include detailed body analysis, all blood panels, a heart stress test like an echocardiogram, an MRI of torso, and full doctor analysis. These comprehensive physical exams typically cost between $4,000–6,000 in the U.S. However, during a visit to Thailand in 2011, I had a comprehensive physical exam at a world-class hospital accredited by the international division of the Joint Commission (TJC) on accreditation in health care (the same organization that accredits U.S. hospitals). It ended up costing about $500.

These savings would essentially take care of your airline tickets and hotel stay for you and a partner for at least a week. It's certainly a cost-effective way to visit other parts of the world. One day for your physical exam and then the remainder of your time relaxing on an exotic tropical beach. Not bad!

REPORT TERMINOLOGY

Affordable Care Act: The Patient Protection and Affordable Care Act (aka Obamacare) was signed into law by President Obama on March 23, 2010. This act is the most expansive health care regulation in U.S. history and will significantly affect the way that doctors, hospitals, and insurance companies operate. The main goal of this legislation is to expand health care insurance to all U.S. citizens through government-designed and -operated insurance exchanges. Citizens that opt out of insurance coverage will face financial penalty (tax) from the Internal Revenue Service (IRS)

Catastrophic Insurance: Insurance policies that cover catastrophic medical care as an emergency safety net. These policies come with high deductibles, which means the monthly premiums are much lower than with other plans.

Medical Concierge service: New business model created by physicians to enroll patients in a premium service plan for an annual retainer fee typically between $1,000–3,000. The premium service usually entails direct cellphone access, longer patient times, same-day appointments, and 24/7 service.

Individual Mandate: The key provision of the Affordable Care Act that requires all U.S. citizens to obtain health insurance coverage or else be levied with a stiff penalty (tax).

Medical Tourism: Traveling outside of your local area for medical treatment. For years, wealthy individuals from foreign countries have been traveling to the U.S. seeking the best care at world-renowned hospitals such as Johns Hopkins, Mass General, and the Cleveland and Mayo clinics. In the past decade, American citizens have begun seeking treatment at hospitals in countries like India, Malaysia, Thailand, and Costa Rica, where the cost is a small fraction of the same treatment in the U.S.

Medicare: Federal health insurance program for individuals 65 or older.

Medicaid: Federal health insurance program for low-income individuals.

Obamacare: Simplified term for the Affordable Care Act coined by opponents and embraced by others, including President Obama.

Private Insurance: Insurance policy that is purchased privately by individuals who are not a part of a group, such as a employers.

Private Medical Lab Testing: Online companies that sell medical lab testing services directly to consumers, which enables people to bypass initial doctor's visit to obtain lab request forms. Such services are especially beneficial to consumers who are familiar with specific blood panels that they track on an ongoing basis.

Single Payer: The term used to describe a national health care system where the government funds health care delivery, rather than private individuals and insurance providers. Great Britain and Canada are examples of health care systems that are differing forms of single payer.

Socialized Medicine: The term that is used to describe national health care systems that are completely regulated and controlled by the national government.

Underinsured: Covered by insurance, but ineligible to certain procedures because they are deemed as having a pre-existing condition. Many orthopedic procedures fall under this category.

Uninsured: Not covered by any form of health insurance.

2 MAKE YOURSELF INVISIBLE TO THE NSA
as Well as All Those Other Snoops, Sneaks & Goons Who Would Simply Love to Plunder Your Privacy!

"But if you have nothing to hide, then you shouldn't have to worry about the government collecting your metadata."

Something is very wrong in America when quotes by Nazi German Minister of Propaganda Joseph Goebbels are used to defend the government's programs. Goebbels, as you may remember, was one of Hitler's principal advisors and confidants.

And today, just like in 1930s Germany, of all the defenses for the National Security Agency's massive spying program, this one is used most often. The apologists might be Republicans that want to be hard on terrorism. Or Democrats who want to find some way to justify president Obama's involvement in the program. Or maybe they're simply your neighbor or co-worker who has never been the political type, but goes along with whatever the government says is OK because they just haven't really thought about it.

People all across the country believe that you need to act like an angel at all times. Failing to do so is your own fault. But let's examine whether you might have something to fear, even if you believe you've done nothing wrong.

As one study showed, there are so many laws on the books in America today that it's almost impossible to go through a day without breaking three laws. And that's counting only the federal variety! Once you add state, county, and local laws that could apply to you, the number quickly rises.

And as any police officer will inform you... ignorance of the law is no excuse.

But there's another important reason why you don't want the government to keep a record of your emails, texts, phone calls, and other online activity. Even if you never break any laws, the social norms of the present might not be the same of the social norms of the future. And the language you use in your online communications that's fine today might be inflammatory tomorrow.

The court of public opinion is always open, and the laws that govern that court change as social norms change.

Who knows what you're saying now that might be construed as offensive or possibly illegal in the future. If you're willing to believe that your private conversations will remain uncontroversial throughout your life, then you might be able to make the case that the NSA's surveillance isn't that bad.

Sometimes you really might not have anything bad to hide. But that doesn't mean you should be fine handing over the keys to your private life. Most people would rather not have their dirty laundry dug up years later, when times change and what was once the norm is now considered taboo.

The mission of this report is to make sure that doesn't happen.

THE FIRST THING YOU NEED TO KNOW...

Before we go into how you can make yourself invisible, it's important to know the inherent limitations of the programs we're about to discuss. For starters, going invisible and using the right encryption tools can only do part of the job. It's important to understand the big picture to make sure you protect yourself properly. Your goal is to use tools that help you change your behavior to make it harder for snoops, sneaks and other online goons to collect information on you without your permission.

For starters, you need to know that you and the computer you're using right now have a specific digital fingerprint. The information that's included in that fingerprint covers a lot of things, from the processor in your computer to the monitor connected to it.

Individually, these things might not be enough to definitely connect you to the computer.

For example, there are many people in the world who are using the same monitor as you. But the number of people who use the same monitor and the same processor is significantly less. Once you add enough variables to the fingerprint (such as the model of your mouse and keyboard or even the type of browser you commonly use), it makes it very easy to distinguish your computer from all the others on the Internet.

And when you do something on that computer that definitely connects you to it — say, order something engraved with your name from Amazon — the metadata stored by the government now has a definitive link between you and your computer.

So with this in mind, it's important to realize that the advice we're recommending can only go so far. You might install government-level encryption on your mobile phone or device (one of our recommendations lets you do just that), but if you order a pizza and have it delivered to your house, you're leaving behind a digital trail.

There's no magic bullet when it comes to making yourself completely secure, but there are plenty of tools to help you get where want to be. Hopefully, that's safely outside the watchful eye of Big Brother.

Now let's begin.

CRYPTOCAT
Online Chats Without the NSA Over Your Shoulder

Twenty years ago, as the Internet started becoming user-friendly to the general population, one of the more popular activities was online chatting. Services like America Online and MSN offered users a chance to chat with strangers all around the world about any topic they could imagine. Instead of going down to your local bookstore to talk about the latest novel, you could join an online discussion and share your ideas with a vast new audience.

But somewhere along the line, the powers that be targeted these online discussions. And while posts on messages boards and forums fall under general Internet activity, live active chat discussions eventually fell under the government's watchful eye.

Internet messages between two users no longer have the intimacy and privacy of early online interactions. Now they're stored and mined like other any data that passes through cyberspace.

Fortunately, there is a way to gain back that lost privacy. Using an open-source program called **Cryptocat**, users can once again enjoy secure conversations through the Internet. RT America, in fact, has even called the program "kryptonite" to the Cyber Intelligence Sharing Protection Act (CISPA). By denying third parties access to the private conversations taking place via the program, it ultimately makes CISPA irrelevant.

Oddly enough, the fact that it's open source actually makes your privacy more secure. The nature of the software allows anyone capable of reading computer code to analyze the program. Privacy experts ensure that the program's claims of privacy are legitimate and act as a safeguard for future versions of the software.

While most people in the United States might use Cryptocat to enjoy secure communications without the watchful eye of Big Brother peering overhead, other groups from different countries could use it for a different reason. Protestors around the world know that they'd be at risk if their private messages fell into the wrong hands. If the demonstrators during the Arab Spring coordinated activities via open networks, the government could easily have cracked down on them before they could organize.

Like any good technology that threatens to upset the status quo, the government has taken note. The Department of Homeland Security (DHS) detained Nadim Kobeissi, the creator of the program, at the U.S.-Canada border in June 2012. Kobeissi claims that it was the fourth time in the previous three weeks that he was questioned by the DHS. The interrogations usually focused on the Cryptocat's encryption algorithms as well as the creator's penchant for censorship resistance.

Unfortunately for the DHS, his detainment ultimately increased the popularity of the program. After the owner tweeted about the latest encounter, there was a spike in the number of downloads for the program. The unintended consequence of the government trying to quell online privacy was an increase in the number of people seeking online privacy.

It's refreshing to find reliable programs created by individuals whose main focus is ideal-oriented. And in this case, the creators of Cryptocat are providing it free to users.

SILENT CIRCLE
Untraceable Cellphone Calls

In our modern world, practically everyone in the country owns a cellphone or some kind of mobile device. It's a piece of technology that allows us to remain constantly connected to the Internet. And while this has created many more opportunities in our lives, if you're not careful, it could leave you exposed to online threats.

Twenty years ago, the majority of families had only one phone line in the house. But today's modern family might have a different phone number for each family member. And each phone number represents an avenue of risk, either from NSA software that collects your information or from potential threats with the technical know-how to tap your private phone lines.

Regardless of the origin of the threat, there is a practical way to secure your cellphone communications. A relatively new Internet startup, **Silent Circle**, made headlines months ago when it released a mobile app that granted the user government-level encryption for all cellphone communications.

The company, located just outside of Washington, D.C., has made it their mission to ensure that the government stays out of your personal affairs.

Which is surprising, considering that one of the co-founders, Mike Janke, is a former Navy SEAL. He came up with the idea after trying to figure out a way for him and his fellow SEALs to make secure phone calls back home to their loved ones. After working as a military contractor, he eventually teamed up with Phil Zimmerman, inventor of Pretty Good Privacy (the same encryption software used by NSA whistle-blower Edward Snowden and *Guardian* newspaper reporter Glenn Greenwald in their initial communications).

The two developed a program that relies partially on a protocol that Zimmerman developed years ago. Silent Circle assumes the role of a service provider. But unlike Verizon, AT&T, and the other major wireless servers, they don't keep any records of calls made. In fact, the technology that the users install on their phones actually prohibits Silent Circle from keeping any records whatsoever.

This is the most critical part of the program. And it's what circumvents the current NSA surveillance network. The system the government has in place copies and stores all metadata that goes across the major carriers' systems. So when you make a call on Verizon, both the phone company and the government gain access to that information.

Silent Circle, however, prohibits itself from ever having access to your information. The company even said that if they were ever served a subpoena for one of their user's phone records, they wouldn't be able to comply even if they wanted to.

As of this writing, the government is not requiring Internet communication programs to be wiretap-ready. In a recent paper, Zimmerman joined with many academics voicing their concern about possible legislation.

The owners of this software are putting their money where their mouth is and creating a system designed with the users' privacy in mind.

There are other messaging services that offer similar strong encryption software. Surprisingly, iMessages from Apple offers users a high level of protection against outside threats. There is a critical difference, however.

While Apple might keep your messages and information secure, they'll still store your information. So in the end, they are the ultimate gatekeepers to your privacy. And when Big Government flexes its regulatory muscles, we believe they'll bow to political pressures, rather than risk upsetting the regulators. Silent Circle, however, does not store your information, meaning your security won't be in the hands of others.

A service as secure as this doesn't come cheap. It's a relatively new program, so it's not surprising that it costs $20 dollars a month to use it.

TAILS AND TOR
Lead the Snoops on a Wild Good Chase Through the Internet

One of the drawbacks of trying to monitor the entire Internet is that there are a lot of people on it. In the United States, 78.1% of the population has access to the Internet. And if you look beyond America, the top 20 countries in the world in terms of Internet users account for roughly two-thirds of the population (about 75% of Internet users).

So it's easy to get lost in the crowd. And getting lost is important if you want to secure your Internet activity.

As we mentioned earlier, the government has various programs in place that can track your Internet signatures and piece together your online identity. When the telephone number attached to your cellphone account calls your doctor, and then that same phone number calls your child's school, data mining programs can connect the dots and tie you to that phone number.

But there's a way to get around that. There is a computer program available on the Internet that allows you to blend in with the crowd, making it more difficult to connect the dots. This may get a little technical, but please bear with us. This could be the most important program you can use to protect your online privacy.

The Amnesic Incognito Live System (**Tails**) is an operating system that helps mask your online activity. The key component of Tails is that when multiple people use it, they all leave the same signature behind. Let's use a quick example to understand it better.

Let's say you and your neighbor are both fishing enthusiasts. You both go to the same sites online to read the latest reviews and articles. If that were the only thing you did on the Internet, when the government recorded your activity, you'd look exactly the same. There'd be no way to tell you apart.

But let's say you and your neighbor went to different high schools. When you both check to see how your old alma maters are doing, you create separate metadata points and, as a result, differentiate yourselves from one another.

But imagine that instead of using two separate computers, you used the same one. So now you both look at the same fishing website, and look up both of your old high schools, from the same computer. Since you shared the same operating system, there's no way to differentiate between users.

Tails is very similar… except instead of just two people using the same operating system, there are potentially thousands. You see, the program enables users to boot up any computer with a preprogrammed DVD or USB thumb drive. When a computer boots up with the DVD inserted or the thumb drive connected, it loads a specific type of operating system. And it's the same operating system for everyone who uses the program.

To make your Internet activity even more secure, it takes advantage of a virtual system of tunnels already in place. This system, called Tor, sends your information through a number of different places on the Internet. This makes it harder for surveillance software to track and monitor you. It's similar to those scenes in spy movies where the star of the film takes a windy roundabout way when he thinks he's being tailed.

Each point in the data's path has limited knowledge. It only knows the point where the information pack just was and the next point it's going to. So as the information moves toward its destination, its digital trail is practically nonexistent.

When using Tails, all Internet traffic is sent through **Tor**'s virtual tunnels, protecting you from anyone trying to monitor your online activity. It's expanding the idea of using the same computer on a global scale.

There are limitations to this program, and it's important to understand them before you use it. This goes back to the earlier discussion about how these security programs can only go so far, and it's up to you to make sure you stay secure. For example, although your online presence might appear identical to all the other users running Tails, if you purchase something and have it sent to your home address, then you've tied your personal identity to that specific activity. The system will still remain intact, and you can slip back into relative anonymity with ease, but something as simple as online shopping can expose yourself.

We recommend that you install the program onto a portable thumb drive so you can bring it with you as you travel.

DUCKDUCKGO
Google for the Privacy-Minded Individual

Sometimes the best solution to your problem is also the easiest one. We've covered a number of programs you can download that will protect your information. Some are fairly simple, and others more technical. But this next solution is hands down the easiest one to implement.

Basically, all it takes is opening up your browser's settings and changing the default homepage and search engine to a more secure website. Google might be the standard when it comes to finding practically everything on the Internet, but there's one website that offers similar search capabilities without requiring you to trade in your online privacy.

That website is www.duckduckgo.com.

When you first go to the site, you'll notice right away that it looks very similar to its Google counterpart. And after your first search, the results will seem very similar to Google and other popular websites. But there's one significant difference.

DuckDuckGo never records any of your personal information or activity.

So while Google regularly tracks browsing history and uses it to compile a better picture of their users (as well as provide a way for the government to record metadata of users), DuckDuckGo doesn't store anything. It's a lot like other privacy and encryption programs that place privacy at the top of their priorities.

The programmers who understand how this technology works know that they are the gatekeepers to their customers' privacy. And they're aware that if their systems become compromised, possibly by online attacks from Uncle Sam, himself, they must hold themselves responsible. And the best way to release them from that responsibility is to remove themselves from the equation.

DuckDuckGo doesn't go any deeper than providing users with a platform to perform searches. In fact, as a result of their refusal to gather personal information of their users, their search results are the same for everyone. As opposed to Google, which customizes results based on a number of factors (such as previous search results and location, to name just a few), DuckDuckGo's responses depend solely on the terms being searched for.

And if the government shows up at DuckDuckGo's corporate offices demanding to see the search results of you or another American, you can rest easy knowing they've hit a dead end.

The real beauty of this solution is that you can use it anywhere at any time. You don't have to bring anything with you, and you don't have to install any software onto the computer you're using. If you want to stop in at the local library to look something up, you can use DuckDuckGo and know that your quick search isn't stored in some government database in Utah. Or that marketers at Google or Yahoo aren't figuring out the next product to put in your ad sidebar based on your last search query.

TRACK AND STORE EVERY PASSWORD YOU'LL EVER NEED

The last solution we have for you is one that we can almost guarantee you'll use every day. Though the other solutions we've offered keep your information secure from the government, this one will protect you from other nefarious online threats that operate outside the boundaries of the law. More importantly, it will give you the security of knowing the passwords that you use every day are safe and secure.

LastPass is a simple program that acts as a vault for any passwords you use. Using open-source encryption software, all passwords are encrypted on your personal computer and can be accessed only via a master password that you control.

An example will better illustrate the benefits of the program. On a given day, you might access multiple accounts to take care of different tasks. You'll probably sign in to your personal email, maybe buy something off Amazon, and check to see how much money you have in your bank account. It's possible that if you don't have your passwords saved, you'll have to enter three different passwords.

Using LastPass, after you open your browser, you log in via the secure add-on and then get automatically logged in to all accounts that require a password. This is especially useful if you're using a public computer or one that multiple people use. You might forget to log out of your bank account, leaving it vulnerable to the next person who uses it. But if you log out of LastPass, you can rest easy knowing that all your other accounts are secure.

One of the most significant benefits of the program is that it will take care of generating secure passwords for you. Normally, the biggest weakness when using passwords is that there is a trade-off between user accessibility and password security. You can make a 16-character password consisting of lowercase and uppercase letters, numbers and special symbols, but trying to remember it and enter it correctly every time is extremely tedious. On the other hand, you can make your password simple, but then it's easier for other people to crack it.

LastPass solves this problem in two ways. First, when you create a new account online, you can use the LastPass' built-in tools to generate a unique, strong password. Second, any passwords you create with LastPass are saved into your online password vault. You can rest easy knowing that your accounts are secure and not have to worry about memorizing long strings of intricate passwords.

Though it sounds obvious, a program is only as reliable as the people who maintain it. A program that offers the highest level of encryption on the market is useless if the government holds all the important keys needed to access the information. LastPass knows this and takes the necessary steps to protect their customers.

They state on their website that the best way to secure your passwords and online security is to keep your personal information out of their servers. This added level of security not only gives you sole control over the keys to your online life, but it prevents outside sources like the NSA from tapping into their servers and finding a backdoor to your information.

Like some of the other programs we've covered in the report, LastPass understands that the key to reliable security is giving as few people as possible access to your information. This way of operating not only offers you an added layer of protection, but it also protects them from potentially exposing their customers to outside threats.

Check out LastPass' website and sign up for a free account.

CONCLUSION

Depending on how much you're willing to commit, you can get a level of online security that will practically make you invisible to the watchful eyes of the Internet. Obviously, that comes with a cost. And it's up to you to decide how much is right for you. These are just a handful of options available online, but they're the ones we feel will give you the best level of security.

If you'd like to continue looking for additional options, we'd recommend taking a look at OpenPGP or PrivacyGuard. These will allow you to encrypt the data stored on your hard drive, giving you an added layer of protection.

We'd like to stress one last time that ultimately, you, the user, are the most important tool you can use when protecting yourself. You can download all the programs we recommend, but unless you understand and respect their limitations and shortcomings, you could easily still expose yourself to the government or other online threats.

For example, did you know that signing in to your computer as an administrator could allow outside threats unprecedented access to your personal files. Yet millions of Americans fall for this trap every day. So even if they take the right precautions and hide their online trail using the suggestions above, they still leave themselves open to an attack they'd never see coming.

Fortunately, with the right setup and a few changes in the way you use the Internet, you can secure your online identity and disappear from the NSA's crosshairs. Good luck.

3 HACK YOUR SHOWERHEAD
Ten Ways to Get Big Government Out of Your Home
Your Home

INTRODUCTION

Long ago and far away, government pretended to do good things for us like build parks, boost income, bring electricity to rural areas, and the like. Today, it is the opposite. It sees its role as restricting and tearing down what the private sector creates — for our own good. This is why it is constantly telling us that it must curb our lifestyles. The regulators restrict what we consume, control what we do, crack down on our ability to live a good life.

If some activity is going well, some new item is making life better, some food or gadget is newly popular, you can be sure that some bureaucrat is plotting to restrict its use or ban it. The ethos of the public sector has completely changed from 50 years ago. Instead of serving us, politicians on both the left and the right imagine that their main role is thinking of ways to control how we live, direct how we spend what money we make, and take away freedoms and rights once taken for granted.

Consider the example of the use of cell phones in cars. When everyone got one, people were just getting used to how to be both productive and safe. Phones started to be made that enabled hands-free talking. New cars were building the functionality into the dashboard. Voice activation was growing more sophisticated by the day.

Just as this was happening, the regulators got involved. Their brilliant idea: ban the whole thing! Because the politicians and regulators had nothing to do with creating the industry, they really don't have any concern over whether the sector thrives or dies. If there is a problem, pass a law. That's always their way these days. They have no more creative ideas other than rolling back progress.

There are certain obvious government regulations that are annoying. Environmental regulations prevent us from developing our property. We must restrict our water usage. We can only create so much trash and then it must be separated by type. We can't travel on planes with wine openers. We can't just hire or fire whom we want. We can't bank where we want. We can't even surf the Internet in peace without fearing that knock at the door.

All of this is true. But in this report I'm more concerned about a second type of government regulation that degrades our lives in ways of which we are not always aware. I've learned over the years how to detect these. If there is something particularly annoying going on, and it doesn't make sense why, look more deeply. You are likely to find a bureaucratic rule of some sort lurking out there. It is usually hidden from public view. The cause and effect are hard to detect. But look hard enough and you find it.

Let me just give one example from the kitchen. Beef and chicken broth and stock that you buy at the store are famously bad. But is this the fault of the manufacturers? Hardly.

Government controls food labeling like Stalin ran the Kremlin, defining precisely what can and cannot be called a stock. The US Department of Agriculture is clear: a stock must have a moisture-to-protein ratio of 135:1. This means that the stuff is mostly water — an ounce of meat to a gallon of water — a result of these government definitions of what is and isn't stock.

But do people know this? Hardly anyone does! We all use stock in our homes. It is the foundation of vast number of meals. We pay and pay to try to get good quality ingredients. In this case, and there are a million more, it is not possible because the government restricts the manufacturers. You can't sell anything called stock that deviates from these mandates. People figure that the manufacturers are the problem, but the real problem is the government itself.

Now, this might not sound like a big deal (actually I think it is). But repeat this scenario a million, 10 million, 100 million times, for every product or service on the market, and you create the equivalent of a Soviet-style central plan that prevents society from improving and degrades our lives bit by bit until civilization itself is under threat. If our washing machines don't work, and our plumbing doesn't work, and we can't get rid of bugs on our property, can't get jobs for our kids, and so on, at some point we will wake up and find progress stopped and rolled back.

It has happened before in other places. Before the revolution in Cuba, the island was a booming, progressing, developing paradise. After the revolution, and socialism controlled the country, all progress stopped. Truly, it literally stopped, as in frozen in time, like the land that time forgot. Nothing new ever happened. Visitors in the 1990s would return with photos that might as well have been taken 30 years earlier except that everyone looked decrepit and depressed. After progress stops, decline sets it, as it did in Russia and China, where lifespans actually fell over time.

This stagnation can happen anywhere, even in the land of the free where freedom is becoming nothing more than a nationalistic slogan. The good news is that once you identify the source of the problem, you have your first clues about finding the solution too. It is not true in every case. Sometimes the bureaucrats have locked every door and thrown away the key. But other times, the answer is right before our eyes, but we never noticed it. These are the cases that excite me because they offer a real and practical way out.

Let's jump right in.

1. ENJOY YOUR SHOWER AGAIN

If you head to the Delta Faucet website, you will see a notice about flow restrictors in their showerheads. "While it is possible to remove flow restrictors from showerheads, we strongly advise against it for several reasons. Flow restrictors for faucets are an integral part of most aerators and it is generally not possible or desirable to remove them."

Is that so? Of course it is not so. Showers in the old days were fantastic. They covered us with water — hot water — and kept us clean. Then government got involved to regulate how much water the bureaucrats think we should be using. The result was the mandate that every showerhead had to be deliberately degraded. The words on the Delta website reflect fear of government and have nothing to do with reality.

Today smaller manufacturers have found profits in advertising showerheads with "removable" flow restrictors. These are best but you can also remove them from the parts you get at the big-box hardware stores. Once I had to actually take a drill to the thing to make it happen but it can be done. And it must be done or else you find yourself running around in the shower trying to get yourself covered with the pathetic trickle that the government has mandated for us.

You might have some vague memory from childhood, and perhaps it returns when visiting someone who lives in an old home. You turn on the shower and the water washes over your whole self as if you are standing under a warm-spring waterfall. It is generous and therapeutic. The spray is heavy and hard, enough even to work muscle cramps out of your back, enough to wash the conditioner out of your hair, enough to leave you feeling wholly renewed — enough to get you completely clean.

Somehow, these days, it seems nearly impossible to recreate this in your new home. You go to the hardware store to find dozens and dozens of choices of shower heads. They have 3, 5, 7, even 9 settings from spray to massage to rainfall. Some have long necks. Some you can hold in your hand. Some are huge like the lid to a pot and promise buckets of rainfall. The options seem endless. But you buy and buy, and in the end, they disappoint. It's just water, and it never seems like enough.

Here is one example of why, from the Santa Cruz City Water Conservation Office: "If you purchased and installed a new showerhead in the last ten years, it will be a 2.5 gpm [gallons-per-minute] model, since all showerheads sold in California were low consumption models beginning in 1992."

And it is not just crazy California. The Federal Energy Policy Act of 1992 mandates that "all faucet fixtures manufactured in the United States restrict maximum water flow at or below 2.5 gallons per minute (gpm) at 80 pounds per square inch (psi) of water pressure or 2.2 gpm at 60 psi."

Or as the Department of Energy itself declares to all consumers and manufacturers: "Federal regulations mandate that new showerhead flow rates can't exceed more than 2.5 gallons per minute (gpm) at a water pressure of 80 pounds per square inch (psi)."

As with all regulations, the restriction on how much water can pour over you at once while standing in a shower is ultimately enforced at the point of a gun.

Manufacturers must adhere to these regulations under penalty of law, and to be on the safe side and adjust for high-water pressure systems, they typically undershoot. If you try your showers right now, you will probably find that they dispense water at 2 gallons per minute or even less. Together with other regulations concerning water pressure, your shower could fall to as low as 1.5 gallons per minute!

A rotten shower creates a rather serious problem for nearly everyone in the country. In the post-war period, Americans fell in love with luxurious showers, just because we could. A long shower with a blasting spray is a sign of prosperity, individualism, and good health. Popular lore holds that Americans are some of the most showered people in the world. If so, part of the reason is that we had great showerheads.

Enter the Regulators

Clearly the regulators, whose regard it as their job to crush luxury and convenience whenever possible, wanted to put a stop to this. That's the reason for the flow restrictors. Forget all that talk about saving water: these restrictions have a negligible effect on overall water use. In any case, whether we use more or less water should be governed by market forces.

To be sure, some companies have tried to get around the regulations by making models with multiple showerheads. This worked for a while because the regulations, if read literally, only regulate the amount of water a per-shower-head basis. But the companies that make double and triple-headed models have also faced investigation and harassment.

But then what can the government do about the length of showers? After all, there is no real way to regulate how much water we use and pay for. Maybe the shower heads have to have timers on them. And maybe the feds need to put up little monitors in our showers to make sure that we have stopped and started them.

You might say that water needs to be conserved. Yes, and so does every other scarce good. The peaceful way to do this is through the price system. But because municipal water systems have created artificial shortages, other means become necessary. One regulation piles on top of another, and the next thing you know, you have shower commissars telling you what you can or cannot do in the most private spaces.

And also consider this. According to the government's own water usage statistic, domestic use constitutes only 1 percent of the total, and that includes all the water we use on our lawns. In other words, whether we use a lot or a little bit of water in our showers means absolutely nothing as regards our nation's consumption of water. Why are they doing this to us then? Just to spread that sense of obedience and misery, I suppose. But has central planning ever been more ridiculous, intrusive, and self-defeating?

The Fix

Most manufacturers adhere to the regulations, and the government has pushed them to make their products ever more useless. But savvy consumers know how to get around the problem. Many people now hack their showers — or customize them, if you prefer. You can take your shower head down, pull the washer out with a screwdriver, and remove the offending intrusion that is restricting water flow. It can be a tiny second washer or it can be a hard plastic piece. Just pop it out and replace the washer. Sometimes it is necessary to trim it out using a pen knife. I've even used a drill.

Using such strategies, you can increase your water flow from 2 gallons per minute to 3 and even 4 gallons per minute. You can easily clock this using a stopwatch and a milk carton.

Using this method, I was easily able to expand my gallons per minute on each shower in my house to an average of 3.4 gpm, thereby recreating that childhood sense of gushes of water pouring down.

2. RECLAIM YOUR RIGHT TO HOT WATER

You may have had a sense lately that something is just not right in your domestic life, not calamitously bad but just bad enough to be annoying on a daily basis and in seemingly unpredictable ways. You are not alone. In fact, a huge variety of personal and social problems trace to a single source.

First an inventory to establish what I mean:

You have the vague sense that your bed linens are not so much comforting you as hemming you in, restricting you and just not breathing as they should;

- To clean your bathtub and kitchen sink requires an inordinate amount of cleanser and bleach;
- Whereas you remember showers that once refreshed you, they now leave you only feeling wet;
- It should be pleasure to put on a bright white crisp undershirt but instead it seems rather routine, dull, even uneventful;
- The mop has a dusky smell of an old rag and you keep having

to replace it to get rid of the reappearing and never disappearing stink;

- Your dinner tonight reminds you of your dinner last night and that night before, and the flavors seem to be piling up into one big haze.

These are just six of the many dozens of typical symptoms of one of the most common household problems in American today. What is that problem? The simplicity of part of the answer might shock you: *your water heater is set at too low a temperature.*

Most people don't want to think about their water heaters. It is a subject we would rather avoid. It just sort of sits there like a steel totem-poll in a dusty closet that is otherwise not used for much because there is not room for much else. The heater itself seems intimidating, plastered with strange insulating devices and warning stickers. It is something to be touched only by specialists. We even fear cleaning behind it, worrying that we will be zapped or scorched.

Sure, we know people who have had to "replace their water heaters" because their water heater went out," but because this has never happened to us, we don't worry about it. Besides, what if it turns out that the water heater has some sort of scary blue flame and a clicking starter or something? Better to leave it alone so that it doesn't become volcanic.

Down with Lukewarm

All of these impulses are wrong. The water heater can be your friend. It can be your greatest friend in your struggle to create and maintain a happy domestic environment. It wants to be useful. There is nothing to be frightened of. There are no blue flames (they are mostly electric now.) A water heater is made to heat and hold water. It is begging you to do something that will change your life from grey to bright white: turn up the temperature!

Chances are that your water temperature is set at 120 degrees. This is the preferred temperature of the regulators. Water heaters are shipped this way and installed this way. The regulations on new home construction mandate it to be this way. Who thinks to change it?

But 120 degrees? Come on. By the time the water leaves the heater and travels through the pipes and hits the air before landing whenever it is supposed to land, chances are that it will fall to 118 degrees. In the dead of winter, with pipes running under the house, it can be even lower.

Think about this: 118 degrees is the temperature at which yeast thrives. It is the temperature for proofing. What does that tell you? It tells you that things can grow at 118 degrees.

In other words, this is too cool! To know what 118 degrees feels like, imagine a bowl of water that you stick your hand in. It is warm, even quite warm, but you don't really have the drive to pull your hand out to keep yourself safe. You can adjust. You know what? Everything adjusts to 118 degrees: germs, viruses, bacteria, dirt, smudge, sludge, stink, dust, and every other damnable thing in the world. All of this lives, even thrives, at 118 degrees.

Revelation 3:16 has it right: "So then because thou art lukewarm, and neither cold nor hot, I will spew thee out of my mouth."

Who came up with the idea that the standard temperature should be 120 degrees? The usual bunch: governments that want to impose a variety of deprivations on you, anti-energy people who think the less technological consumption the better, environmentalists who want to stamp out all things bright and beautiful, litigious lawyers who have intimidated heater makers, and safety freaks of all sorts.

Some of these people can be extreme. They say we should eat our own garbage, invite bats to live in our attics, and refrain from killing mosquitoes in the marsh. They are the ones who gave us toilets that don't flush and shower heads that don't spray. They seem to think we should all go around dirty and dissatisfied, and that anything resembling clean, neat, and, well, civilized has to be stamped out.

These people are always worrying about the risks of life, but what about the health risks of living in squalor of their creation?

The Fix

Here is how you can defy them all in one fell swoop! Turn your temperature up to 130 degrees. How hot is this? Contrary to the claims, it will not scald you. Imagine again a bowl full of water. Put your hand into this temperature and you will say: "Yikes!" or Ouch!" or "Yeow!" and pull it right out and shake your hand in the air. However, it leaves nothing red, no burns, nothing awful. It is just what used to be called hot water before the lukewarm crowd changed everything.

How does yeast respond to 130 degrees? It dies. Bread bakers know this. You know what else dies? All the icky things mentioned above. They all die mercifully quick deaths at this temperature. Clean clothes! Clean sinks! Satisfyingly hot showers! Comfortable sheets! Clean-smelling mops! Plates that come out of the dish washer without dinner build-up on them! All of this awaits your act of defiance.

A brief note on shoes. Have you ever bought a new pair because your old ones…stank? Of course they did. Your socks are not getting clean. They infect your shoes. Oh sure, try to keep it at bay with Dr. Scholl's. It won't work. A shoe stink sticks forever. You thought you had a physical disability, and embarrassing foot odor problem. Nope. It's your hot water heater.

How to fix all this? It will take less than a minute. If your temperature dial is in the open, good for you. Turn it to 130 degrees or higher. There is a reason these tanks go up to 170 degrees. I read a manual for a dishwasher that says it wants water of 145 degrees. When I was in the dish-washing business, you had to use heavy rubber gloves just to get near water. So be it.

If your dial is covered, ignore all stickers and scary warnings about scalded babies. Take off the steel plate that covers up the setting. Remove the Styrofoam. There you will find a tiny little dial. Use a dime or a screwdriver and give the dial a teeny tiny little turn over to 130 degrees.

The benefits will start within hours. Within a day, you will experience the greatest increase in your standard of living since your gas grill and automated sprinkler system. Your new life begins with a comfortable and happy sleep, a blasting hot and refreshing shower, a crisp T-shirt and clean socks, followed by breakfast on a plate so clean it squeaks. Even cleaning up breakfast will be pure pleasure: the sink gleams, the floor has never been cleaner, and your mop will end up as fresh as the day you bought it.

Indeed, with a water heater set at 130 degrees, all is right with the world — at least that part of it that you can control.

Even if the whole world is conspiring against civilization, you can preserve your part of it with the smallest turn of a screwdriver.

3. TURN THE TRICKLE INTO A TORRENT

The water pressure issue in a home is a major factor in how your faucets, showers, and toilets work. Low pressure causes sediment to build up in the pipes. It causes clogs. It causes breakages. All our sewage systems are designed for massive quantities of water to rush through on a constant basis, and so it should be. What is the prime example of the high civilization of ancient Rome? Its aqueducts that rushed water from place to place, making sure that we could bathe and wash and live a decent life.

In the last 20 years, regulators have been using secretive strategies to reduce the water pressure in our homes. Once there were no regulators on our systems at all. Now they are mandatory.

No house in the country can be legally built without them. Today, 50 and 70 pounds per square inch is considered normal pressures for residential uses. However, when the manufacturer ships the item, regulators mandate that they are preset at 45 to 55 pounds per square inch. In other words, they must be adjusted from their default setting.

How often does this happen? During the housing boom, contractors were building them so fast that homes often retained that low setting. The results can be an amazing annoyance but most people don't know the source. They blame the faucet, the washing machine, the water dispenser on the fridge, but the real problem is not inside the house. It is outside at the water meter under the iron grate.

The Fix

Whether you do it yourself or have someone else do it, it should be turned up to at least 75 to 85 pounds per square inch. A setting of 100 is standard for how high it can go. You will be warned that this is too high and that this can damage your plumbing. Plumbers I've talked to in private say that this is bunk. It takes pressure of 150 or higher to actually bring about problems. Nonetheless, 80 is probably plenty but think of it: the valves are shipped and installed at half the proper pressure.

It's up to you to change it. Now, to be sure, some people are rather alarmed to discover what is under that grate. It can be full of bugs and weeds and standing water. Blech. There is a solution. Next time a plumber comes over to the house, just politely ask him to take care of the problem of low water pressure. Now, this request will initially alarm him. The guild knows its regulations and all plumbers worry that they will get in trouble for unauthorized changes in your system. But the truth is that there is nothing to prevent them from making this adjustment, and most will agree after warning against it.

Go back inside the house and be amazed at the difference. The spray on the faucet will be better, and probably it will begin to cough up some build up. The same effect will present itself in every area of the house.

This can even make the house smell fresher. Toilets and plumping, for example, are intended to have high amounts of water running through them. That gets rid of the smell. Low pressure can cause a house-wide stink that will immediately go away when the pressure is increased.

It's a small change that will make domestic life vastly more livable. It's not illegal, but I wouldn't go out of my way to tell the regulators what you are doing.

4. GET THE GOVERNMENT OUT OF YOUR LAUNDRY AND DISHWASHER

I'm old enough to have a vague memory of clothes so white that they were called bright. This happened despite the absence of additives — the ridiculous varieties of sprays and bottles and packets that festoon our cabinets today and that we throw into the wash to try to boost the cleaning power of our pathetic machines and increasingly useless laundry soap. If this stuff is so wonderful, why isn't the detergent made from it?

Then I experienced an amazing blast from the past. I added a quarter cup of trisodium phosphate (TSP) and otherwise "treated" nothing. The results were nothing short of mind-boggling. Everything was clean — clean in a way that I recall from childhood.

Next came my confrontation with the local dry cleaner, which I've used for years. I explained what happened and how puzzling it is that by using TSP I was able to clean my clothes more thoroughly and perfectly than his commercial service.

He was not shocked. He completely agreed, though sheepishly.

I pointed out that TSP, which is a natural element discovered in the 16th century, is amazing not because it cleans — it needs soap to do its thing — but rather because it rinses, whooshing away all dirt, oil, stains, as well as all leftover detergent. Bleach whitens but it ruins fabrics, and that's not good. What is needed is a good rinsing agent that leaves clothes not only perfectly clean but also smelling fantastic. TSP does it, and that's why it has long been an essential ingredient in laundry soap.

Once again, he agreed.

Does he use it? No. And why not?

It is not "commercially viable," he said.

How can this be? It is not expensive. It is freely available at the hard-ware store in the paint section. If something works, the laundry service pleases its customers more. That means more business and higher profits. Isn't the goal to clean clothes well and do a good job for customers?

Yes, true, he said, but, again, TSP is not "commercially viable." He politely deferred all further questions to the Dry Cleaning and Laundry Institute, whose website provides no information at all to nonmembers. However, the Laundry Institute did answer my email. It admitted that trisodium phosphate produces cleaner laundry.

Bingo. Cleaner laundry. Cleaner than what? Anything else. Not "commercially viable" means that governments will no longer permit laundries to clean your shirts. You can add TSP at home — government hasn't restricted that yet — but commercial houses cannot. However, the Laundry Institute did say that "there are other ways to achieve a clean shirt." What are they? He didn't say. He said: "You will have to do some leg work to find a cleaner that meets your needs."

My needs? My needs are for clean clothes, same as the laundry needs of the whole of humanity since the beginning of time. The whole purpose of laundries is to meet that need.

Here's the problem, however. The goal of the regulators who regulate the laundry is not to improve your life. It is to wreck your life a bit at a time by pressing increasing numbers of restrictions and mandates upon private producers.

Conspiracy of Silence

One of these mandates has removed TSP from detergent — and with catastrophic results. No one wants to talk about this. There is a major hush-hush culture here because business, understandably, doesn't want to face a consumer backlash, and government doesn't want to acquire the reputation for being the civilization wrecker that it truly is.

These kinds of regulations are capable of driving an entire industry into the ground, as people with the intense desire for clean clothes — the very people who are willing to pay for laundry services — increasingly resort to home cleaning and ironing. An entire step in the structure of production is eliminated, as laundry autarky replaces the division of labor, which is the driving force of cooperative human effort.

It's no wonder that the industry wants no talk of this problem. Its very raison d'être is under attack. If laundries can't clean clothes, they have to shut down.

Does government care? If you read between the lines in the almost-candid moments of government statements, you can see what is going on here. In 2009, Clive Davies, a product engineer with the EPA, granted an interview with the New York Times that focused on home products. You might wonder what a product engineer is doing working for the government rather than the private sector. This interview shows why. Every one of the questions he is asked concerned the effect of home products on the environment. Not even one actually probed the essential question of whether the products actually work.

Mr. Davies's job is to decide whether to affix a supposedly valued designation to products: Designed for the Environment. It's pretty clear that anything that actually cleans, washes, or scrubs probably can't earn the designation. An empty box that claims to be detergent stands a better chance of gaining the government seal of approval than a detergent that actually works.

Then we get to the end of the interview, in which he is actually candid about the goal: the elimination of detergents (meaning the elimination of clean). Davies concedes that this would be the best possible result. And what does he recommend instead? Vinegar and elbow grease" — the old-fashioned phrase for "scrub harder."

Thus spoke the government. That's the future as these bureaucrats see it. It's a future of elbow grease, meaning manual labor unassisted by any products of free enterprise like machines and detergents that work.

It's a future in which our clothes are dirty, we have no soap that works to wash our bodies, our dishes are full of gritty film, our floors are grungy, our windows are smudgy, everything more or less stinks like vinegar, our toilets don't work, our trash is hurled in a pile out back, and vast amounts of our time are spent scrubbing things instead of reading, singing, writing, or conversing. It is a future just like the long-ago past, complete with wash tubs, wash boards, and outhouses — along with their attendant dirt, disease, and deprivation.

The main issue here is that Americans (Europeans too) are having their living standards systematically degraded by regulators who apparently hate our modern conveniences like washing machines and want to drive us ever more into an impoverished state of nature.

And don't tell me that phosphate-free dish soap works just as well. It's a laughable claim. If you buy some phosphate and add a tablespoon to the load, you enter a new world once the washer is finished. Things are actually clean like you might remember from childhood.

The sales of new home appliances have soared over the last five years, according to industry reports. The data are not broken down by type, but I'm willing to bet that quite a few washing machines have been sold to unsuspecting customers who had no idea that the real problem was with the detergents, not the machines. Hardly anyone I have spoken to has understood this problem, but all confirmed the fact that their clothes are not getting clean.

The ban on TSP in laundry soap that took place in the early 1990s, apparently codified in a 1993 law. The idea, or the excuse, was to stop the increased growth of algae in rivers and lakes (phosphate is a fertilizer too), even though there are other ways to filter phosphate, home use contributes virtually nothing to the alleged problem, and there is no solid evidence that plant growth in rivers and lakes is a harm at all.

In any case, consumers gradually noticed that stains were becoming more stubborn than ever, and thus did a huge new range of products start appearing on the market. These products permit you to treat your clothes before you wash them. Today our cabinets are filled with such products — spray and wash, bleach pens, stain removers, boosters of all sorts — and we use them by the gallon.

Does anyone stop and wonder why such products are necessary in the first place, and, if they are so good, why aren't they in the detergent so that the whole of the load gets clean and not just the treated part? The reason, most fundamentally, is that the formula for detergent was changed as a result of government regulation.

The difference wasn't obvious at first. But as time has gone on, other changes began to take place, like the mandates for machines that use less water with "top loading" model, along with mandates for tepid temperatures of water in our homes. In the end, the result is dramatic. It all amounts to dirty, yellowing clothes.

This is the exact opposite of what we expect in markets, in which products are ever better and cheaper due to innovation, expansion of the division of labor, and competition. But with government regulation, the results are deliberately the opposite. We pay ever-higher prices for shoddy results.

Do we see what is happening here? I can detect very little in the way of public knowledge, much less outcry. In the old Cold War days, I recall wondering how it was that the Soviet people could have put up with state-caused impoverishment for decade after decade, and wondering why people didn't just rise up and overthrow their impoverishers. Now I'm beginning to see why. If this all happens slowly and quietly, there is no point at which the reality of cause and effect dawns on people.

One final note on my conversation with my dry cleaner. He gave me the heads-up that the main ingredient used for dry cleaning, perchloroethylene, is not long for this world. California and New York are considering bans, and the rest of the country comes later. After that, it's all over, and the last one to leave civilization will have to remember to shut off the fluorescent light.

This is the whole trajectory of life under government control. They are the predators; we are their prey. And this isn't just about clean clothes. It applies to every regulation, every tax, every expenditure, every stupid war, and every monetary manipulation. Everything government does comes at our expense, and the costs are both seen and unseen.

The Fix

A quarter cup of real TSP (don't buy the fake thing) combined with your usual laundry soap will yield wonderfully clean clothes, provided you were suckered into buying one of the government-approved front-loading models of machines. Clean clothes require 1) lots of water, 2) lots of heat, and 3) detergent with phosphates. Then you can throw all those other silly products in the trash. The bleach, which absolutely wrecks cotton, can go too. Thanks to the government, you can only find in the paint section of the hardware store.

The Attack on Clean Dishes

The whole problem began in 2011. Dishes used to come out of the dishwasher hot, beautiful, dry, and clear as a bell. I never thought much about it. The dishwasher worked. You put them in and they came out clean.

One day that started to change. My first thought was, well, I guess I have the wrong washer and this one is old. So I bought another one. Presuming that a new one would surely be fine, I didn't pay much attention but after a few weeks, I noted the same issue. The dishes were coming out with dusty rings on them and strange particles. I was having to rewash them. As I noted over the coming days, the new washer was even worse than the old one.

I was kicking myself for not having checked Consumer Report before buying, but then I remember my experience with clothes. Surely it could not be the case that the same ridiculous problem is present in the detergent I use for dishwashers. Surely not!

In this case, I could find no evidence of any regulation that required soap companies to take out their phosphates. But as I went through the aisle at the store, there I saw it in tiny print, again and again: no phosphates. A bit more looking and the answer became obvious. It turns out that the soap companies had been threatened with a push to eliminate phosphates. This would have destroyed their entire product.

So rather than face that regulatory regime — inflexible and violent — they all agreed to remove them on their own volition. Why? Because removing them from consumer products would allow them to retain them for commercial products. As a result, right now, consumers can only buy inferior detergent. But if you are a company or restaurant you have special access to brands that do contain phosphates.

It's been different for millions of others. People just do not know. So they spend money on new machines. They buy ever more detergents. They curse free enterprise for giving them bad products. Or they just adjust and downgrade their living standards. Instead of using a dishwasher, they hand wash their dishes, wasting time and engaging in unseemly tasks that economic development is supposed to eliminate.

Once again, the regulator is hidden here. There is no ban in place on phosphates for dish washing soap. But the companies who make this soap have learned how to anticipate regulations even before they are in place. They decided to degrade their product before the government, with great public attention, forced them into it. But there have the power of government today. It can destroy civilization through threats alone.

The Fix

TSP once again comes to the rescue. Add a tablespoon to the dish washer, and, like magic, the good old days come back. It will happen immediately. You will never have trouble again.

5. HOLD ON TO THOSE TOILETS FOR DEAR LIFE

My order at my favorite Chinese takeout was taking too long. I stopped into the men's room. There I witnessed a common scene: the modern toilet disaster. An otherwise clean business had a restroom calamity on its hands, one so grim that I hesitate to describe it.

The conjectural history is not difficult to reconstruct. The toilet apparently had trouble flushing. There was a plunger by the toilet, of course, as we see everywhere today. The toilet was plunged to get rid of the obstruction, while the obstruction itself spilled all over the floor and stuck to the plunger too.

The customer probably left the ghastly scene in a rush. Management knew nothing. But now customers were coming and going into this bathroom, surely losing all inspiration to eat or order food.

It would be easy to blame the restaurant owners. What is with these people and why can't they at least have a clean restroom? But reacting this way would be unjust. The hidden hand behind this unsanitary calamity is the US government. The true origin of the mess was not in the hour before I arrived but back in 1994, when the Energy Policy Act (passed in 1992) went into effect.

This act, passed during an environmentalist hysteria, mandated that all toilets sold in the United States use no more than 1.6 gallons of water per flush. This was a devastating setback in the progress of civilization. The conventional toilet in the US ranges from 3.5 gallons to 5 gallons. The new law was enforced with fines and imprisonment. Hardly anyone even knew that this was happening. The whole course of human history has sought ways to remove waste products from our domestic environment, and, suddenly, without notice, the government decided to intervene to make it more difficult to live a clean life. It's an outrage!

Toilet Smuggling

For years, there was a vibrant black market for Canadian toilet tanks and a profitable smuggling operation in effect. This seems either to have subsided or to have gone so far underground that it doesn't make the news. I've searched the web in vain for evidence of any 3.5 or 5.0 gallon toilet tanks for sale through normal channels. I wonder what one of these fetches in the black market. This possible source has no prices and an uncertain locale.

The toilet manufacturers, meanwhile, are all touting their latest patented innovations as a reason for the reduced hysteria surrounding the toilet disaster. I suspect something different. We have all gotten used to a reduced standard of living — just as the people living in the Soviet Union became accustomed to cold apartments, long bread lines, and poor dental care. There is nothing about our standard of living that is intrinsic to our sense of how things ought to be. Let enough time pass and people forget things.

So let us remember way back when:

- Toilets did not need plungers next to them, and thank goodness. Used plungers are nasty, disease carrying, and filthy. It doesn't matter how cute the manufacturer tries to make them or in how many colors you can buy them. In the old days, you would never have one exposed for guests. It was kept out in the garage for the rare occasion when someone threw a ham or something stranger down the toilet.
- Toilet paper was super thick and getting thicker. None of this one-ply nonsense.
- You never had any doubt about the capacity of the toilet to flush completely, with only one pull of the handle. The toilet stayed clean thanks to five gallons of rushing water pouring through it after each flush.

These were great cultural and civilizational achievements. In a state of nature, the problem of human waste and what to do about it is persistent. Do the wrong thing and you spread disease and misery.

Indoor plumbing since the time of the ancient world has been a sign of prosperity and human wellbeing. Indoor toilets that flow into a sewer have been around since 1500 B.C., but every new settlement of people in a new area presents the problem anew. In rural America, indoor toilets weren't common until the 1930s. That today everyone assumes them to be part of life is a testament to the creative power of economic progress.

What we have in these regulations passed since the 1990s is therefore a step backwards from a central aspiration of mankind to dispose of human waste in the best possible way. We have here an instance of government having forced society into a lower stage of existence.

Government has reduced us as people to the point that we either have to enter the black market to get good sewage or come to terms with living amidst periodic spreading of human waste all over our domestic and commercial environment.

Again, this is wholly unnecessary. Capitalism achieved something spectacular in waste disposal. Government came along and took it away from us. That's the story in a nutshell.

Today, every toilet company touts its latest innovations to overcome the problem. There are high-pressure blasters that run off electricity, designed to force a paltry 1.6 gallons of water through fast enough to make the difference. They are shockingly loud and scary. There are new shapes of tanks and new flow mechanisms that are said to compensate for the calamity, but this works only some of the time.

Each of these innovations is patented — meaning that a successful project cannot be copied and improved by other companies. So even if these are improvements, their distribution is limited and the successful aspects of them are not extended by others, for fear of patent lawsuits. The entire market is hobbled.

The result is an entire society of poorly working toilets and a life of adjustment to the omnipresence of human feces, all in a short 20 years. Our toilets are dirtier, and combined this with lower water pressure and you find them breaking down ever more. Thanks so much, Congress!

Of course the environmentalists are in on the whole project. They started telling us back in the 1970s that our large tanks were sheer waste. We should put bricks in them to save and conserve. If you didn't have a brick in your toilet, you were considered irresponsible and a social misfit. Eventually of course the brick became, in effect, a mandate, and finally toilets were reduced to one third of their previous size.

Back then, it was just assumed that toilet manufacturers cared nothing at all about wasting water. Surely there was no rationale at all for why they consumed five gallons per flush as opposed to 1.6 gallons. This is just capitalist excess and down with it!

Well, think again: there was wisdom in those old designs. The environmentalists didn't account for the present reality in which people typically flush twice, three times, or even four times during a single toilet event. Whether or not this ends up using more or less in the long run is entirely an empirical question, but let us just suppose that the new microtanks do indeed save water.

In the same way, letting people die of infections conserves antibiotics, not brushing teeth conserves toothpaste, and not using anesthesia during surgery conserves needles and syringes.

Here is the truth that environmentalists do not face: Sometimes conserving is not a good idea. There are some life activities that cry out for the expenditure of resources, even in the most generous possible way. I would count waste disposal as one of those.

It is also possible that some people just like to get their kicks out of spreading misery and making it impossible for us to enjoy a clean and prosperous life. Like Puritans of old, they see virtue in suffering and would like to see ever more of it. It sounds perverse, but such an ethos does exist. And clearly, government doesn't care in the slightest.

There are many tragedies associated with the toilet calamity. There are private embarrassments at guest houses and disgust at every turn. Many of the customers at that Chinese takeout probably blame the owners, who themselves are probably mystified as to why toilets in communist China probably worked just fine but in capitalist America are throwing filth all over their restaurant.

It's the hidden hand of government that has mandated this leap back to barbarism.

The Fix

For many people, there is no way out. New homes come with models that work better than they did ten years ago but none are as good as models from the 1980s and before. For people in older homes, you have an opportunity. Never replace your own toilet tank. They are highly valued in the marketplace of course. But they also add value to your home. There is simply no way you can replace them with anything better.

And while it is true that old tanks are virtually unavailable, there is never any harm to getting an eye out for them. Of course you have to install them yourself. Plumbers are forbidden by law to do this professionally. Yes, this is what it has come down to in the "land of the free."

Many people, however, have had success in ordering directly from Canada or Mexico. That's right: toilets outside the U.S. are typically large capacity. Can you order these legally? Yes you can. You can even pick them up and drive them across the border. You might experience some harassment but the government can't actually stop you, at least not on grounds of your toilet. It is legal to bring them in for non-commercial uses. However, you will need to install them yourself. And the shipping charges can be outrageous.

6. ADD YEARS TO YOUR AIR CONDITIONING UNIT

Ah, Spring, the time when the landscape appears as if it were painted by a great artist, when the birds make music of symphonic quality, and when the very air we breathe feels air conditioned. That last point is particularly important, because it is only true so long as we are outside. If we are inside, it is a different matter altogether.

Most of the year, indoor air is fabulously fresh, clean, and circulating at the right temperature, thanks to the greatest source for clean wonderful air: not the Clean Air Act but central air conditioning and heating. When people say, hey, turn on the air, it is literally true. We hardly open windows anymore, which (not being Mr. Outdoors) I think is fine in principle.

But in the Spring, the air goes off. It is no longer cold enough for heat but it is not yet warm enough outside for the air conditioner. The thermostat tells the machine to stay put. You could turn on just the blower, but who thinks of doing that? So the air just sort of sits there, dormant and still. It is the right temperature, but it is not moving.

You might not notice this at first. But once you focus on it, you suddenly realize: I'm suffocating! This is precisely the revelation that hit me two nights ago. For two weeks, nights had been oddly miserable. I wasn't too hot or too cold, just oddly and unidentifiably uncomfortable. I would wake somehow unrested. Am I sick? Am I getting old? Finally it hit me. The only circulation in this room comes from human breath!

This room needs a fan running. On it came, and with it, life itself. The night was suddenly glorious, clean, and happy. All dreams were dreamy. I awoke and there was once again music in the air, the feel of flowers, the sound of birds (metaphorically of course). The fan had brought the Spring indoors.

Then I began to notice something. This problem isn't limited to the bedroom. It afflicts virtually all indoor space. In the Spring, with neither heater nor air conditioner, indoor air begins to sink into a stultifying blechiness. If you are sitting in the same spot, you are breathing the same air again and again.

My office needed a fan too! I turned it on to the same effect: the flowers appeared, the birds sang, the air moved! Suddenly my day has become as glorious as my night, filled with rapturous, Spring-like freshness. The fan! God bless it.

In any case, we might as well get used to fans because government regulations over the last decades are trying to wreck our air conditioners and central heating units. If you have had one break in the last few years, you know this. Or maybe you know the outrageous expense but not the reason Government regulations on refrigerants and power efficiency have caused the cost of air conditioning to soar. It can cost up to ten times what it did ten years ago.

Curious as I am about these matters, I ask every air-conditioning expert I know about this subject. They all confirm it. While the costs of things tend to go down in a real free market economy, the opposite has been true in air conditioning. Repairs will normally cost $500 plus. New units can be $2,000–$5,000. Nor do they last as long as they once did.

The Fix

Manufacturers are permitted to make units that use only so much electrical power. They must choose among the features in which to allocate this energy ceiling. The lighter, more efficient" parts tend to break more easily than they once did. This means that you have to replace the units more often than you did in the past.

By the way, it is the same with refrigerators. Manufacturers have to choose among features and are forced to make products that are less robust than they once were. This means that we must use them less in order to get value from the products. With refrigeration, this is extremely difficult. But with air conditioning, there are some options. You can use a fan to drastically reduce the burden on your units.

Let's just say that the manufacturers went along with all the new regulations in hopes of actually selling more units over time. I've not done the research to prove this but it wouldn't surprise me. One way out is to secede from this round-robin approach of buy and replace, buy and replace. This simple solution will add years to your units. And you can have the satisfaction of knowing that in the smallest way, you have help subvert the racket of the industrial-regulatory complex.

H.L. Mencken defined a puritan as someone who has a haunting fear that someone, somewhere, may be happy. It is true with regulators too. They have a haunting fear that someone, somewhere, might be using technology in a way that brings comfort and convenience to life. They are seeking to crush this at every turn, and air conditioning is high on the list. They want to you to pay the big bucks just to keep yours running.

The least we can do is preserve our units as long as we can, not paying the big bucks to feed their perverse desire to wreck our comforts.

7. APPLY A NEARLY BANNED SOLUTION TO DRAIN CLOGS

Let's return to the issue of water in the house. The scene is quite dreadful. The water pressure is low so that pipes don't clean well. The tank is undersized so that the flush doesn't work well and the toilet gets and stays dirty. The inside parts of the tank break easily because they are not moving fast or well because there is too little water going through the tank. The same is true of the shower and the sink. Everything is economized so that the pipes don't get the workout they need to stay cleanly functioning.

What is the result? Far more shower, toilet, and sink clogs than you can remember from ten or twenty years ago. You know this too. Think about all the hotel showers and sinks that you have seen that are completely clogged. It is really disgusting. You have the shower running for two minutes and then find that you are standing in a pool of water. You brush your teeth only to find a swamp mess in the sink. This is common, even in the nicest hotels. It all traces to the many ways in which government has degraded our plumbing.

It happens in your own home. So you go to the hardware store. You know from experience that liquid drain openers do not work so well. You recall that powders work better. Best of all is old fashioned lye. It gets hot as can be and destroys nearly every clog you can possibly make. You have to be careful with it because it can seriously harm your skin but, hey, we are adults here.

But two years ago, I began to notice something odd. The grocery store stopped carrying it. Then one hardware store stopped carrying it. Then every big-box store removed it from the shelves completely. I searched and searched the Internet to find out some reason. I figured that there had to be some regulation, but, no I found nothing. Finally I asked the purchasing manager at the hardware store what happened to the lye. The answer surprised me. Apparently it was all removed after some news reports that lye was being used in some illegal drug-making process.

Given all the publicity and regulations that had followed other cases like this, the stores stopped carrying it to protect themselves from liability, to avoid bad publicity, and to forestall the inevitable ban that would happen in the wake of such publicity. This was once again a case where the commercial sector responded to the mere prospect of a threat of regulation.

The Fix

Fortunately, there is still time left to buy lye online. That window might not last for much longer. For now it is there, and it has never been more necessary. A few cans of this stuff will last many years, and save you money on worthless products sold in the grocery store.

Let me just pause to express some outrage. Government wrecks our toilets. They wreck our ability to pipe water into our homes. They try to foist tepid water on us. They put flow stoppers on our faucets and showers. And then when the whole mess begins to back up and threaten even the basic sanitation of our homes, they put in place a system that makes retailers afraid even to sell us products to fix the resulting disaster.

As I said at the outset, government once imagined that it was improving our lives. Now it is the main culprit in degrading our lives and forcing us backwards in time. Why do we put up with this? We should not.

8. KILL THE BUGS

When I was a kid, you could know an insecticide by its smell. It had that certain scent that projected a message: all nasty bug things will die forever when faced with this potent poison. There is comfort in the smell. Bugs and insects are nasty. They are dangerous. They once wiped out of Europe's population in successive rounds of the black death. Even in the 19th century American South, insects caused terrible diseases called yellow fever. Today in Africa, they still kill millions.

Insects are the only things on this planet that have killed more humans than governments have killed. We dare not treat this subject lightly. And yet nearly all the information we receive today from the regulators and environmentalists speak nothing about the benefits of pesticides. They talk only in the broadest terms about the danger they represent to "insects, animals, and/or humans." Note the weasel term here "and/or." Of course they represent a danger to insects! That's the whole idea.

That we can even talk about banning pesticides is a testament to their success. Mankind has been menaced by pests for all of human history. It is rather ridiculous to imagine that we are menaced by chemicals that took away one the deadliest of killers. But such is the way politics works.

Our tendency to underestimate the dangers of nature while overestimating the dangers of chemicals stem from several factors. An increasingly urban population thinks that "nature" is more like a pretty public park than the disease-ridden swamp that our ancestors feared. The ideology of "back to nature" is spreading due to environmentalist mania. Now that the pesticides have worked to eradicate disease and massively increase crop yields, people imagine that they can be banned without cost.

Partly due to lobbying pressure, the list of banned pesticides is growing. The movement began in the 1970s and has grown exponentially.

Most of the bans in existence were enacted in the 2000s and industry and consumers face ever few options today. Even when the West Nile Virus struck the United States in 1999, there was a crazy outcry about the notion that we might actually do something to eradicate the mosquito population. How many people have to die before people figure out that stopping the development of bug eradicating chemicals might be a bad idea?

So that we consider the plus side of chemicals, hear B. Lomborg The Skeptical Environmentalist (Cambridge University Press, 2001). "If pesticides were abolished, the lives saved would be outnumbered by a factor of around 1000 by the lives lost due to poorer diets. Secondary penalties would be massive environmental damage due to the land needs of less productive farming, and a financial cost of around 20 billion US Dollars'."

As true as this statement is, it comes nowhere to expressing the full reality of situation. But this isn't about trying to get you to love or use pesticides. Most of us have contracts with bug spraying companies that treat our homes with chemicals far stronger than we could get at the hardware store.

But let's say that we really do have a bug problem, really are dealing with serious issues just outside the door and want to actually get rid of the problem. There are ever fewer options. Even the legal chemicals are not carried in hardware stores as they once were.

This is true of the most widely used pesticide in the United States, Malathion. This was the chemical that brought West Nile under control.

It is useful against many forms of pests and it is a major reason for how farmers keep the fruit fly under control. I use it in my home. I'm not a chemist or expert in this area but I can tell you this much: it has the same smell from childhood that just says, this stuff kills bugs.

The Fix

So if you want to use this chemical at home, you are not likely to find it. However, many people don't know that it is actually widely available online. You can find it from many dealers online at Amazon for very cheaply. How long will this be true? It is hard to say. The push to ban it is well organized even though there is not a shred of evidence that it harms people.

If this goes the way of other chemical pesticides, it could be banned nearly overnight. At that point, prices will skyrocket and you won't be able to fine any. You will be unable to control a mosquito invasion or some other problem we do not yet know about. The time to stock up, then, is now. Getting pesticides before their banned is not something that the rice-and-beans survivalists think much about. The truth is that under the right conditions, a good pesticide is all that stands between your family and grave illness and even death.

9. STOCK UP ON SOON-TO-BE-BANNED PRODUCTS

It's been eight years since the feds took aim at nasal decongestant. Under George Bush, a normal part of everyday civilized life became a criminal act, namely the over-the-counter purchase of Sudafed and many other products containing pseudoephedrine. You can get it now, but it is seriously rationed. You have to present your driver's license and no one without one may purchase it. The limits on quantities you are permitted to purchase fall far below the recommended dosage, and buyers rarely know when they are buying too much.

The rationing and criminalization of this product appeared as part of the Patriot Act. The replacement drug phenylephrine is far less effective on noses but more effective in Washington: the company that makes it, Boehringer Ingelheim, spent $1.6 million lobbying Washington in 2006 and the same amount the year before. The makers of the drug everyone actually wants are diffused and spread all over China.

Pseudoephedrine was targeted in the name of the drug war because apparently you can use it to make methamphetamine. Since the near ban, there are indications that production of the drug has gone up, mostly due to smuggling in Mexico. Even a quick Google demonstrates that the gray market is thriving.

I've written with sympathy toward those who have been caught in the legal tangles; many buyers are not actually doing anything wrong. Anyone who attempts to buy it is treated like a criminal and one never knows for sure when one is buying more than the legal limit. In several cases I've highlighted, people have bought without the intent to manufacture drugs but were ensnared in any case. In other cases, people have been asked to buy for friends who may or may not have been plotting to make meth. Still other cases involve shady figures with criminal records and suspicious associations who are thereby discredited and hounded by police and judges.

In my view, every person who is ensnared deserves to be defended. Their rights are being violated. One lady in my own community faces 20 years in jail solely for buying 4 boxes in a 12-day period. News reports suggest that she is a bad person for many other reasons, and, for that reason, there has been little public sympathy for her — in the same way that people under alcohol prohibition were snagged on alcohol grounds even though the motivation for getting them was different (could be taxes or something else).

Something as serious as laws and jails should be used for punishment of those who infringe on person and property, not for self-medicating. If this lady is bad, she should be punished for things she did wrong, not for some trumped-up reason.

In any case, as with all stupid laws like this, the innocent are eventually harmed. It's strange how most people are willing to give the police and the courts the benefit of the doubt, and pretend as if the system somehow knows something that we do not know. Anyone hauled off to jail probably deserved what is coming to him, even if we don't know the specifics. People should do a better job at staying out of harm's way, of being beyond reproach. Don't play with fire and you won't get burned — this is how people tend to think of these cases.

They are blaming the victim. Somehow I suspect that the same sentiments were pervasive even in the worst totalitarian states. By the time people wake up to the reality that the law and the law enforcers are the problem, it is too late.

To get the real stuff, you have to go to a drug store, not just the convenience store. Then you have to ask. Then you have to show your license. Then they ask how many you want and you get the sense that you are begging like an addict. Then you sign some national registry. Then later, one presumes, you are checked to make sure that you are not buying more than your officially allotted amount.

Don't lose what you have because then you can't get more. Nor can you keep some at the office, some in the car, and some at home. No, you must guard the stuff with your very life, lest you run out and are denied more by the Stuffy Nose Czar.

Before 2005, you could buy as many Sudafed packages as you did Big Mac sandwiches, and the police didn't care. Now, your 30-day allotment is nine grams. So this seems like it would be enough, but what if you are buying for two people or an entire family, or lose some, or give them away to a friend, or they fall to the back of the cabinet, or you're out of town? And how can you possibly track precisely how much you have purchased?

There is now an air of fear and threat in the process of fixing a clogged nose that wasn't there a few years ago. When I bring this subject up to people, they say, "Oh, that's plenty of Sudafed for one person, so stop your kvetching." To me, this illustrates how regulations and rationing have a way of changing the subject from principles to practicalities. What if there were a rule that said that you can only purchase 30 Triple Whoppers from Burger King per person per month? Would we say, "Oh, no one needs more than that? "

Perhaps we would, but that is not the point. The point is that this is a violation of rights. Rationing of all types represents an egregious imposition on our right to choose. It weighs down daily life with arbitrary threats and increases the role of coercion in society — and this is true whether or not we actually bump up against the limits.

What was lawful only a few years ago now gets you written up in the papers as a drug dealer. It ruins your life.

In my view, all drugs should be completely legalized. People tell conjectural horror stories of Meth Inc. distributing the stuff online, but they don't shake me in the slightest. The people who use the stuff would still do so, and those like me who have no interest still would not. The key thing is that the dangers to person and property would be dramatically reduced, and essential rights to do things like unclog our stuffed noses would remain intact. As the New Yorker pointed out about Portugal's experience with legal drugs, "drug use has significantly diminished. Portugal now has the lowest rate of lifetime marijuana use in people over 15 in the E.U and lifetime heroin use among 16–18 year olds fell from 2.5% to 1.8% between 2001 and 2006."

The real horror is the prohibition, which has brought about a dark despotism that everyone pretends not to notice. It now even affects our ability to innocently medicate our way out of the common cold.

What do to? If your family uses Sudafed, it is a good idea to buy slowly a bit at a time, and do not wait until the cold season when the kids and parents all get the same ailment at once. This is the work-around. This way you don't get on anyone's flagged list of panic buyers and you still medicate your family.

Soap and Bulbs

I've seen various notices that anti-bacterial soaps are also on the list. The crowd of lobbyists that essentially hates all of modern life has this notion that they really make our hands too clean, that they cause bugs and bacteria to grow resistant (hey, this is a race that mankind can and must win!), and that there is really nothing wrong with the smell of human sweat and fungus.

As for the rest of us, give us the freedom to use anti-bacterial soap. How much longer will it be around? It is hard to say. Maybe the campaign will fail and the threat will go away. If this follows the trend, we will wake one day to find that this product has vanished from the shelves. I'm betting on the latter.

Let us now address the great light bulb controversy. I've come to loathe fluorescent lighting. Maybe you agree. Maybe you disagree. The point is that in a free society, people should have choice, and it is incredibly obvious that consumers want the freedom to buy incandescent light bulbs. This is what governments all over the world are working to destroy.

There is fascinating symbolic meaning to this. The light bulb was one of those hinge-of-history innovations that changed everything. The night lit up. An innovation of mankind finally conquered darkness. Those who resent progress and hate human happiness have never quite gotten over it.

Every time I go to the hardware store these days, the shelves are short on incandescent bulbs. Clearly consumers are stockpiling them, and rightly so. Liberal commentators make fun of these habits, claiming that there is no pending ban and that this is really some kind of paranoia at work.

The truth is that the ban has been on and off again for many years now, with the legislative and regulatory pressure going decidedly in the direction of banning them all. Wikipedia sums up the current and very confusing state of things:

> In December 2007, the federal government enacted the Energy Independence and Security Act of 2007, which contains maximum wattage requirements for all general service incandescent lamps producing from 310–2600 lumens of light.

> However, these regulations never became law, as another section of the 2007 EISA bill overwrites them, and thus, current law, as specified in the U.S. Code, "does not relate to maximum wattage requirements." The efficiency standards will start with 100-watt bulbs and end with 40-watt bulbs. The timeline for these standards was to start in January 2012, but on December 16, 2011, the U.S. House passed the final 2012 budget legislation, which effectively delayed the implementation until October 2012.

It is a heroic thing that a few Members of Congress tried to save the bulb but this provides little comfort to those of us in the real world that love them and depend on them. I would personally rather sit in the dark than under a naked fluorescent bulb. Apparently millions of others agree with me here, because consumers are stocking up on regular bulbs as never before. As well they should.

Reflect on the tragedy here: we are dependent upon a gang of elected charlatans to protect us from the depredations of unelected regulators. Liberty is not safe under these conditions. Even our ability to conquer darkness with warm light is threatened.

The Fix

But you can outsmart them. Now is the time to stock up on necessary drugs, soap, and light bulbs. This is not to prepare for natural disaster or economic collapse. This is to anticipate the unnatural disaster of government bans products that make our lives better.

10. DON'T LET THE MAN STEAL YOUR LEGACY

You are a writer, composer, painter and you imagine that copyright is crucial to protecting your intellectual property now and after your death; this is how to immortalize your legacy. It turns out that the opposite is the case. Now and at your death, your best strategy for maximizing your impact on the world is to give your intellectual property into the commons of the culture. Otherwise, you risk dooming your works to near-permanent obscurity.

Why is this a case of getting government out of your life? Copyright is a government invention. It didn't exist in the ancient world, in the world of St. Thomas Aquinas and Voltaire, in the time and country of Shakespeare, Bach, Mozart, and Beethoven. In 19th century America, schoolkids were taught by and read books from England because their copyrights were not enforceable here. In fact, copyright only became universal at the turn of the 20th century, just as big government began to tax, regulate, and largely wreck what free enterprise had created in the previous centuries.

The purpose of copyright is to restrict access, not guard value. The value of an idea is hinged on the degree to which it permeates the culture and society. Copyright does the opposite. With enforcement growing ever more intense these days, we are seeing the digital takedown of books, images, music, and movies, so that they are relegated to obscurity. This is true not only of new works but old works still cover by the law.

Consider this recent case of composer Igor Stravinsky, whom many regard as the greatest of the 20th century musicians. He lived from 1882 to 1971. Many of his works have been part of the standard fare of city orchestras and recording groups for many decades. But because of a strange decision by the Supreme Court in early 2012, many of his works will no longer be played.

The Supreme Court permitted his works — and millions of others written and composed between 1923 and the 1970s — to be re-copyrighted to match international law, which freezes ownership of works for the lifetime of the author/composer plus 70 years. That new legal status will permit publishers to sue any orchestra that does not pay the licensing fee that can be in the six figures. That means it won't be until 2041 before Stravinsky's works are accessible in live performance again. After all, who benefits from this sort of decision? Not Stravinsky or even the Stravinsky estate. The composer himself wrote with a mission to bring an artistic message to the world. Copyright law has now censored him forty years after his death! The winners here are the publishers who hold the "rights" to the works that are in charge, profiting when people are able to pay and otherwise happy to keep the treasure nicely monopolized and buried for as long as possible.

And again, millions of others are in this position too. Books, music, and ideas of all sorts are being kept from public view. For years I've worked with authors and estates to try to bring novels, non-fiction, poetry, music, and other art into print only to find access blocked by deep-pocketed publishing houses that happened to have been sold the legal rights. Millions of works are now buried and lost, and this is happening ever more.

Under this system, the author, whether living or dead, has no rights at all. The estate is often confused and conflicted. The end result is that the works don't see the light of day. The creator wanted to make a dent in the universe of ideas but the law is stopping this from happening.

This is a form of cultural destruction wrought by the law and the courts. It is truly tragic. When Google put up its online art archive and its book library, there was a gaping hole. The 20th century is not represented. It's like the whole century fell into a black hole. The reason is copyright. It is the same in the commercial marketplace. New research shows that books from the 1870s or today more available than books from the 1970s. There is a gigantic gap of 80 years in which the reprint editions are very few in number.

Copyright Does Not Protect You

Many people imagine that copyright has something to do with protecting the value of intellectual property and guarding it from somehow being looted. They imagine that protecting copyright after a person's death is the right thing to do, in the same way that it is right to care for the home of the deceased or his financial legacy.

But this is entirely wrong. A house or a bank account is based on scarce goods that would otherwise depreciate if not owned and protected by someone who cares. An intellectual legacy is capable of being infinitely copied and distributed even as the integrity of the original is wholly maintained. Ideas are non-scarce goods that need ownership once they are released.

An intellectual legacy can be universalized only if it is universally available. The only way to assure that this can happen is to keep it out of copyright. For maximum exposure and use, ideas must enter "the commons," that is, be wholly accessible to all of humanity. There can be no doubt that this is what Stravinsky would have wanted. It is being stopped because both men made a mistake. They permitted their works to be copyrighted in their lifetimes and these copyrights persisted long after their death. Their legacy is now being looted by private publishers who restrict access thanks to government regulation.

Another relevant story here. I know a case of a Canadian composer who had published thousands of pieces of music in his lifetime, all using copyright. After he died in the 1960s, he was largely forgotten. Then in the age of the Internet, his works began to circulate again, available for free download in many places around the world wide web. His reputation was coming back. His works were being performed. A biography was being written. A new generation was discovering his amazing artistry. His music was becoming part of the culture of our times.

Precisely as this began to happen, a big institution got wind of his growing popularity. They sent a delegation to the composer's 92-years old daughter. They paid her money, told her that they would make sure to protect her father's legacy, and got her to sign all the relevant legal documents. The daughter wanted to do the right thing. She thought she had.

But in the week after the deal was sealed, the new owners immediately got to work. They wrote every website that was distributing unauthorized copies of the music and threatened them with legal consequences unless the free downloads were removed. That was the great contribution that the composer's daughter had made possible! Nearly overnight, this composer's work vanished without a trace. His comeback was stopped in its tracks. Whether and to what extent his works are heard from again is entirely up to the new publishers.

For this reason, it is generally a huge mistake for any author, painter, composer, or poet to name a "literary executor" to his or her works. By law, this ends up being one person, and it is a person that the deceased more or less trusted to do the right thing. But what does the power of executor really mean? It is a power to exclude access. The deceased artist doesn't really think of it this way, but that it is what it comes down to: the person so named will work to stop people from using the work pending a payment that the executor himself or herself names.

It is inevitable that the executor will imagine himself to be the successor in some sense, but this is never really the case. The person is usually some sort of hanger-on who was trusted just because he or she was in closest proximity during the real creator's dotage.

The end results are almost always comical or tragic, depending on your perspective. The heir's goal is to extract as much money as possible from licensing agreements, thereby spreading ill will in association with the name legacy. The executor has every incentive to keep the ideas he represents in short supply so as to drive up the price and the royalties. Finally, the executor will attempt to "ride the coattails" into fame and fortune (think Yoko Ono to John Lennon).

These days, everyone is a writer, a creator. You have an interest in seeing your literary or artistic legacy live on past your death. There are two steps. First, never sign a publisher's agreement to give an institution the rights to your works. They will keep them for the rest of your life plus 70 years. You will have lost all control even to quote your own works. Never mind that the company says you are the copyright holder. This means nothing. See the fine print. You have no rights.

The Fix

There is an easy way to avoid the prison of copyright. Publish your material in what is called the Creative Commons (pull it up with a quick Google). This special legal status was created so that authors could get credit from their work, profit from it, but avoiding losing their rights. There are many levels of Creative Commons. The one I recommend is the Attribution license 3.0. This means that you and others can use the material but must attribute its creator.

The second step is to adjust your will so that you *clearly distinguish between tangible and intangible property*. Name no executor of any of your intangible intellectual property. Instead, state explicitly that all your work should be part of the commons of the culture. If there are aspects of it that you do not want to have in this status, you can always destroy them or forbid them from being released. But everything you do want released should be part of the common property of mankind. This will give it the best chance of taking flight and influencing the world after you are gone. This does not preclude you from naming someone you trust to do the releasing after your death but you need to be extra sure of the language here: insofar as it is possible, never die with conventional copyright attached to your works unless you want your legacy tied up in a thicket for 70 years.

So many great painters, writers, composers, and singers have made the mistake of trusting government institutions (and private parties that use such institutions) with their legacy. It never turns out well. We can't do anything about the problems that keep great art out of the commons but you can do something yourself to make sure that your own work never sees the terrible fate of Stravinsky. Publishing and giving to the commons is a wonderful way to get government out of your life, your death, and making it sure it stays that way long after you are gone from this earth.

Conclusion

The government has wrecked many things that can't be fixed. I only recently figured out the precise regulations that cause our lawn mowers to stop working properly. Yes, the reason is due to federal regulations. I could fix it myself if I had a machine shop and a blowtorch but I do not. So I live with the results of a deliberately degraded quality of life.

That's a short history of the last several decades. Government is un-raveling civilization. Fortunately government is doing this more slowly than private markets are building civilization. The progress we see all around us is due to this more than anything else. It's a race between them and us. How long can we keep outrunning them? I don't know the answer to that, but I know this much: insofar as I'm able, I will keep trying.

4 STARVE THE BEAST:
14 Still Legal Ways to Slash Your Taxes in 2013 and Beyond

In George Harrison's classic Beatles song, "Taxman," one line goes, "There's one for you, 19 for me," speaking from the perspective of the taxman. This was in reference to the fact that the success that he and his bandmates found through their music pushed them into the top "superbracket" of the English progressive tax system at the time.

For all the hard work the Fab Four did throughout the world, they were "rewarded" with an incredible 95% tax on all their earnings over a certain level. When asked about the inspiration behind the song, Harrison's answer was blunt.

He said, "'Taxman' was when I first realized that even though we had started earning money, we were actually giving most of it away in taxes. It was and still is typical."

The greatest rock and roll icons of our time might have had trouble keeping what was theirs, but that doesn't mean you have to suffer the same fate. And though the current tax system in the United States is nowhere near as oppressive as the outrageous progressive tax system of England, the tax burden currently levied on middle-class families is more than it ever should be.

This is one of the reasons why we've put this report together. In preparing it, we poured over countless government regulations, read through thick tomes of tax preparation books, and scoured the Internet for any useful tax deductions and tax credits that range from out of the ordinary to well off the beaten path.

In this report, we assume you're probably well aware of all the popular tax tricks. Like deducting medical expenses, or tax credits for sending your kids to college. We didn't bother putting any of those here.

As you're about to see, this report is about the niche tax dodges that your accountant probably doesn't even know about. More important, they're legal tax dodges that the IRS wants to keep quiet. Because they're probably aware that they exist. And they know that if these tax dodges become public knowledge, they'll start to see their funds slowly dry up.

But before we begin, it might help calm your fears to understand the government's methods in determining whether or not you get audited. A *Forbes* article from March 2013 helped put things in perspective by laying out the chances various incomes have of getting that dreaded letter from the IRS:

Type of Return: Individual	No. of Returns Filed	No. Audited	% Audited
Total	*143,400,000*	*1,481,966*	*1.0%*
Income <$200,000, no Schedule C or E	*79,000,000*	*308,000*	*0.4%*
Income <$200,000, Sch. C or E <$25,000	*10,400,000*	*122,000*	*1.2%*
Income <$200,000, Sch. C or E <100,000	*1,400,000*	*50,000*	*3.5%*
Income <$200,000 but <$1,000,000	*4,400,000*	*140,000*	*3.2%*
Income >$1,000,000	*337,000*	*41,000*	*12.1%*
Type of Return: Corporate	**No. of Returns Filed**	**No. Audited**	**% Audited**
Total	*2,000,000*	*33,000*	*1.6%*
Assets under $1,000,00	*1,200,000*	*11,000*	*0.9%*
Assets >$1,000,000 but <$10,000,000	*19,000*	*4,000*	*2.1%*
Assets >$10,000,000	*58,000*	*10,000*	*2.1%*
Type of Return: Pass-Through	**No. of Returns Filed**	**No. Audited**	**% Audited**
Partnership return	*3,500,000*	*16,7000*	*0.5%*
S Corporation return	*4,400,000*	*22,000*	*0.5%*

If you think you might be at risk when tax season rolls around, keep reading to learn some possible ways to lower your tax burden.

THE "EARLY INHERITANCE" TAX DODGE

This dodge is one of our favorites. It not only gives you the opportunity to lower how much tax you'll end up paying at the end of the year, but it also provides a way to transfer property to your children without it being taxed away. And it's all legal.

You'll need to own both the house you live in and the land it's built on. That sounds redundant, but when it's all explained, it will make sense.

First, you'll need to set up an irrevocable trust with your children as beneficiaries and an independent trustee overseeing everything. Once that's done, draft a deed that separates the land from the house itself.

Here's the most important part: You need to *gift* the land, but not the house, to the trust for your children. Tax regulations permit each parent to give up to $14,000 to each child, tax-free. On top of that, they each have a lifetime gift tax exclusion of up to $5.12 million. As long as the value of the land doesn't exceed $10.24 million (the combined gift tax exclusion of both parents), you can transfer the land to your children and not have to worry about taxes.

Like we said earlier, this report isn't about the obvious dodges everyone knows about. There's a reason you need to separate the house from the land.

Now that the trust owns the land underneath the house that you still possess, it will then offer you two options. You can either move your house elsewhere (which is unlikely), or you can pay a lease rental fee. Clearly, paying the lease rental fee makes the most sense for most of you.

And that's where the "early inheritance" dodge pays off.

You can deduct the rental fee you pay at your higher tax bracket, while the income your children's trust receives from the "rent" will be taxed at their lower bracket. Let's say you pay $1,000 in rent and are in the 28% bracket. The deduction will save you $3,360. Your children might only be in the 10% bracket, meaning they'll owe $1,200 dollars from the income they collected.

You and your family pocket the difference of $2,160! And the best part is that it can be done year after year after year.

THE PET DEDUCTION NO ONE KNOWS ABOUT

This is a tax deduction that a lot of people could claim, but few do, because hardly anyone knows about it. It's one of those tax regulations that was probably written quickly, without much thought, but can reward countless families who qualify.

Almost everyone knows that if you get a new job, you can deduct your moving expenses if it's far enough away from your current home. It's probably a common question that tax accountants ask their clients each year because it's so easy to take advantage of.

But we're not interested in that.

Did you know that if you have to move for a new job, not only can you write off your moving expenses, but you can also write off moving expenses for any *family pets*? It doesn't matter what kind of pet they are, how old they might be, or what breed they are. If you have to pay to move your family pet with you across the country, you're allowed to deduct any related costs.

And in some cases, they can add up. We've seen reports of some airlines charging up to $250 for a plane ticket for a dog. If you have more than one pet in your family, the costs associated with bringing your pets with you to your new home/job/life might be close to $1,000.

Depending on which tax bracket you're in, that could mean a couple hundred dollars off your tax bill, in the end.

THE AMISH TAX HOLIDAY

Back in 1954, when the Social Security Administration first began taxing and covering "agricultural workers," the Amish took issue with Social Security's forced participation. The program, also known as Federal Old-Age, Survivors, and Disability Insurance, is a pretty brash affront to the Amish credo. Not only are the Amish famous for "taking care of their own," but the whole concept of insurance goes against their faith. As people extremely serious about God's plan, they don't take kindly to a government-mandated hedge against His prerogative.

So in the late '50s, the Amish started their resistance to Social Security. Naturally, they were quiet and reasonable about it. Some put money into a bank account and insisted the government place a lien on it. At least that way, some Amish thought, they weren't voluntarily paying into the program. Others signed a petition and sent it to Capitol Hill. But naturally, the IRS paid no attention and kept insisting that FICA taxes be remunerated… until eventually, many Amish just stopped paying.

The whole conflict came to its climax in 1961, when the IRS went after one of these "delinquents," Valentine Byler. Long story short, he owed over $300 in back Social Security taxes, so the IRS repo'ed three of his six horses. No kidding. (At one point in this fiasco, *Reader's Digest* reported a judge berating the government's representatives, "Don't you have anything better to do than to take a peaceful man off his farm and drag him into court?" Apparently not.)

To the Amish's credit, they kept resisting the FICA tax, insisting that it violated their First Amendment right to practice religion free of government interference. Byler's story, as you can imagine, was a real hit with the media, and within a few years, the IRS caved under public pressure. In 1965, the government passed a law that allowed U.S. citizens to opt out of Social Security.

Of course, only a small minority of Americans can legally stop paying Social Security taxes and strike their beneficiary status. In order to qualify for the IRS' exemption, you must:

- Convince them you are part of a religion that is "conscientiously opposed to accepting benefits of any private or public insurance that makes payments in the event of death, disability, old age, or retirement"
- Have a ranking official of this religion authorize that you are a true believer
- Prove that your religion has been established — and continually opposing insurance — since at least 1950.

If you do manage to get an exemption, know that you might be trading in your freedom to drive a car and own health insurance.

HEALTHY RELATIONSHIPS FOR YOUR TAX RETURN

In our research, we came across one tax guru who came up with the idea of claiming any children you have in your household as independent contractors, and then deducting their weekly allowances from your tax return. This sounds like a clever idea, but there are a few problems with it. Namely, you need to actually have them perform a real service for the business you own.

But there are ways to take advantage of this very idea. If you do happen to own a business and have a relative or significant other living with you, you can hire them to work for you. For example, a man hired his live-in girlfriend to manage and oversee several rental properties that he owned. She bought furniture for the different units and oversaw any repairs that needed to be done.

In the end, he successfully deducted up to $2,500 dollars of the $9,000 he paid her to manage his business. Unfortunately, he wasn't able to claim the household chores she did as a business expense.

But you really can't blame him for trying.

THE "OTHER" BENEFIT OF VOLUNTEER AND CHARITY WORK

If you're not aware that you can deduct certain expenses related to volunteering, you should look into it. It's a great way to lower your tax burden while also giving back to a charity you care about. Most of the time, the deductions are used to cover things like gas and things you might have bought for a specific activity.

But in my research, I came across another handy volunteering-related tax dodge. And it's especially handy if you have small children in the household.

If you have to hire a babysitter to watch the little ones while you're volunteering, the IRS will allow you to consider what you pay as a charitable contribution. I suppose the government sees this as just another extension of the deductions afforded to charity and volunteer work. Regardless, something like this can help lower how much you'll wind up owing at the end of the year.

THE PREVENTATIVE AND EXPENSIVE MEDICAL EXPENSE YOU CAN DEDUCT

Throughout the course of our research, medical deductions seemed to pop up everywhere. There are so many rules and regulations regarding medical and health services that it's a treasure trove when looking for ways to chip away at the taxes you owe.

For example, even though most health insurances don't cover it, you can deduct the entire cost of a full body scan if you pay for it out of pocket. The best part about this dodge is that you don't even need a doctor to approve it.

A quick search on the Internet shows that the prices of these body scans range from $600–3,000. For someone in the 28% tax bracket, this could potentially save you around $840.

Whether or not this will change after Obamacare fully goes into effect is anyone's guess. (We didn't have time to dig into the 1,000-page bill.) But as of right now, you can take advantage of this medical tax dodge.

More importantly, it could help you catch a problem early on, before it gets worse.

YOUR PREFERRED TAX-FREE INVESTMENT

Neil George, a colleague at Agora Financial and editor of *Lifetime Income Report* and *Total Income Alert*, told us about this next tax dodge. It's not necessarily in the same category as a medical deduction or a tax credit, but we like it because it's an interesting way to collect tax-free revenue. The best part about it is that you don't have to jump through any loopholes to take advantage of it.

I'm talking, of course, about municipal bonds. Specifically, Neil suggests three municipal bond funds below.

These funds are unique because they're used to fund various municipal projects throughout the United States. And unlike other bonds that are available, they're exempt from taxes in the state in which they're purchased.

First is the **AllianceBernstein National Municipal Income Fund (NYSE:AFB)**. When it comes to bonds, this management company has some of the best muni investment pickers, and the numbers prove out. It has earned investors 115% for the past 10 years and 6.17% for the past year — while paying a monthly dividend check yielding 5.8%.

If you factor in what you'd lose to taxes from a conventional dividend payout — assuming a tax rate of 35% — AFB's yield equates to an effective yield of 8.91%.

Second is the **BlackRock Municipal Income Trust Fund II (AMEX:BLE)**. The monthly dividend is currently yielding 6.13%, which, adjusted for taxes, equals a tax-equivalent yield of 9.46%. And the return for the year is 12.44%.

Third is the **Nuveen Quality Income Municipal Fund II (NYSE:NQU)**. This is run by one of the best known in the municipal market management businesses. It yields a current rate of 5.12%, giving a tax-equivalent yield of 7.80%. The fund itself is up over 7.77% for the year.

As with all good things… there is one thing to consider. The tax-exempt benefits extend only to the dividend checks that these funds send out. If the price of the stock increases, you'll be liable for any capital gains taxes you would incur.

Even with this, we still think the fund is a great opportunity.

WHEN IS A SWIMMING POOL MORE THAN JUST A SWIMMING POOL?

When it's a potential tax deduction that could save you thousands of dollars at the end of the year.

You should know right now that you might not qualify for this deduction. But when we came across it, we knew it was something we had to include. It's the kind of idea that's right up the *Laissez Faire Club*'s alley.

In certain circumstances, you can deduct a portion of the costs of installing a pool, as well as maintenance costs associated with it, as a medical expense. In the story that we came across, a man was diagnosed with emphysema, and his doctor recommended that he swim more to improve his breathing and overall health.

In response to his doctor's advice, he installed a pool in his house and deducted some of the costs when it came time to pay the taxman.

The way the tax code is written, however, prevented him from deducting the entire amount. Understandably, installing the pool in his home increased the value of his property. The IRS only allowed him to deduct the difference between the cost of the pool and the added value to his property.

For example, an endless pool might qualify as a deductible medical expense. It's designed to create a flowing current so that a person can swim continuously without worrying about hitting the end of the pool. It's great for cardiovascular exercise as well as strength training for weak knees or joints.

A pool like that might cost around $19,000. Installing one in your house might add an additional $10,000 of value. In this case, you'd be able to deduct the $9,000 difference between the two amounts. If you find yourself in the 28% tax bracket, this could save you over $2,500.

IT'S NOT JUST A HOBBY TO YOU

It could potentially be a tax-deductible activity. The IRS has some strange rules when it comes to income made by activities typically deemed as hobbies. But if you qualify, you could potentially deduct any related expenses you might incur. In fact, it's even possible to deduct up to 100% of all income related to your hobby.

Just make sure you make it clear to the government that you're not intending to make any profit with your hobby.

We'd say that'd be a nice surprise, not to mention a great excuse when someone says your hobby is just a waste of time.

"MAIN STREET LOAN SHARK" DODGE

Why should Wall Street and the big investment banks with all their government connections get all the tax breaks when loans go bad?

That's the first thing that popped into our heads when we came across this next tax dodge. According to the IRS, if you keep the right documentation, you might be able to write off any personal loans that go bad. You need to keep in mind that the documentation is the most important part. Loaning a friend $20 for lunch and then finding out he has no intention of ever paying you back won't fly if you get audited.

So if you're in the habit of lending friends and other acquaintances money, it might be a good idea to take a couple easy steps to cover yourself in case they can't pay.

MEDICAL GAS MILES

This one is small, but it could apply to almost every taxpayer in America, so we included it. Practically everyone who pays taxes knows that they can deduct medical expenses. But few people are aware that you can include in those medical deductions certain transportation expenses.

According to the IRS, if you use a car to transport yourself or your dependents to doctor's offices, hospitals, outpatient facilities, or anything along those lines, you can deduct 19 cents for every mile driven.

There is one stipulation, however. The mileage must be "primarily for, and essential to, medical care." So if your mom or dad is in the hospital, you can't deduct the mileage when you go to visit with the rest of your family.

Remember to keep accurate records of your miles if you plan on using this tax dodge.

THE "GOOD SAMARITAN" TAX DODGE

If you're like many Americans, when a loved one needs constant care and attention, you might be the one who takes care of them financially. Though the current tax system does a lot of things wrong, it does allow people who take care of their elderly or sick parents to claim certain deductions.

In many cases, the elderly or sick parent's own income might be too much for them to qualify as a dependent. But if you provide more than 50% of the financial support to take care of the parent, any medical expenses that you pay for can be deducted when it's time to pay taxes.

If you and your siblings share the financial responsibility, there are ways to get around the 50% threshold.

Taking care of an elderly or sick parent could be one of the most difficult things you do in your life, so it's nice to know there are ways to lessen the financial burden you might encounter.

TAX-FREE HOUSEHOLD INCOME

Every year, millions of Americans pass up the opportunity to put one of their most valuable assets to work for them. Most homeowners don't realize that there is a provision in the IRS tax code that allows them to rent out their primary residence for up to two weeks (14 days) and not have to declare the income they receive.

The important thing to remember is that once you go over that time period, all income earned, which includes the initial two weeks, becomes taxable.

For people in specific areas, this could be a huge opportunity. Imagine having a house near a major sporting event, like the Final Four, the Super Bowl, or the Augusta National Golf Club where they play the Masters. Wealthy sports fans or celebrities would be more than willing to pay top dollar to stay at a place accessible to these events.

But this doesn't apply only to sporting events. Back in 2009, when President Obama was first sworn into office, his inauguration was such a hot-ticket event that hotel rooms throughout D.C. quickly filled up. Savvy D.C. residents who didn't want to bother with the headache of all the people in the city quickly offered their apartments and houses to inauguration attendees. A weekend getaway could easily be paid for by renting out your apartment for one night. And all that money earned was tax-free.

There are sites on the Internet that cater to this kind of informal rental arrangement. Using a system that tracks and rates both renters and landlords, it matches travelers from all over the world with alternative accommodations.

But the benefits don't have to stop there. Coupling this dodge with charitable contributions might allow you and a charity/church you support to benefit in the long run.

Consider this scenario. Instead of renting your house to a golf enthusiast, rent it to a local charity for a monthly event. Charge a fair rate, comparable to what other hotels in the area are charging. For example, let's say you ask for $500. You do this once a month, so at the end of the year, you're still below the 14-day limit. You've collected $6,000 dollars. At the end of the year, you donate $7,000 to the charity for all the hard work they've done for the community (and not because they rented your house).

What's the end result? The charity is better off. They're up $1,000. And after you deduct the $7,000 as a charitable expense, assuming you're in the 25% tax bracket, you save $1,750. Factor in the extra $1,000 you threw in and you're up $750 in the end.

Everyone is better off (though I'm sure there are some government bureaucrats who would think otherwise).

THE TAX TREASURE BURIED IN YOUR HOUSE

The way tax regulations are currently written, you might be able to claim a huge tax deduction on your house. If you've been living in your home for more than two years, any gains you make from its sale could be kept tax-free.

Before you go out and throw a "FOR SALE" sign on your front lawn, there are some things you should know. Like every good tax dodge, there are certain criteria you have to pass before you can take advantage of this opportunity.

The most important one is that you're not just trying to buy a house, renovate it, and sell it for a higher price. The IRS doesn't look too kindly on house flippers. With that in mind, the house will have to be your primary residence for at least two years. They don't have to be two consecutive years, but you will have to prove that it was where you lived if you ever get audited. Additionally, this must be done at least five years prior to the sale of the house.

Using this dodge every five years could result in thousands of dollars of deductions for you and your family.

5 THE BITCOIN BIBLE:
The Safest and Easiest Ways to Buy, Sell, Store, and Speculate

WHAT IS BITCOIN?

The world of Bitcoin is today one of the most promising, confusing, erratic sectors of the emergent world economy. So it will be for years to come because Bitcoin is in its infancy. Currently, it operates as digital payment system. Its efficiency far surpasses any other method of sending and receiving money. Its operation makes PayPal seem old fashioned and clumsy.

But its potential is actually far greater. It seeks to be a competitor to all existing government currencies. Indeed, it could eventually replace them. In time, Bitcoin and other "crypto-currencies" could reinvent the monetary and financial world from the ground up — on the basis of human choice rather than government imposition. But for now, the primary users and enthusiasts of this nascent digital currency belong to the young generation raised in a world swimming in computer code.

How can we know it has a future?

Consider the modern trajectory of digital innovation. In the last 20 years, letters have become email, television has become YouTube, and telephones have left the wall socket and become pocket video phones. This is the digital revolution, and it has been accomplished by the free market, not by government. It was not a "plan"; it is something that came about through trial and error through the commercial marketplace.

Bitcoin is in a similar position to what email was like in 1990 or so. Hardly anyone understood how it worked or why we would need it. Most email addresses were long numbers like 34243920@compuserve. com. There were only a few commercial services around. You had to dial up and connect to send and receive. Servers crashed. Messages were awkward because people didn't know how to use email. Then the spam problem came. That was followed by the terrible problems with viruses.

The purpose of Bitcoin is to serve as a digital-age payment system, evolving one step at a time into an independent money to compete with that forced on us by the nation-state.

At any point in the evolution of email, there were people who doubted it would amount to anything at all. It would never replace the letter, people said. It was insecure, we were told. It was too much trouble, people thought. But gradually, over time, nearly every problem with email was solved, one by one. The technology stabilized. People discovered the great truth about software: A great technology is still great, even if the services using the technology need time to stabilize and get their act together.

Over time, of course, email won the day. Now it is indispensable. And there are new iterations that are making gigantic inroads, from Facebook and Skype messages to smartphone SMS systems. We navigate the world with hand-held devices that speak directions and give real-time traffic data. We now take it all for granted. It wasn't always so. Not even the science fiction cartoon The Jetsons imagined the existence of email. But now it is a reality of the modern world. No one thinks a thing about it.

The next step is in this evolution is obvious: Money too needs to be reinvented. For a hundred years, the dollar has been essentially nationalized by the government and the central bank. Now there is market pressure for a money that leaves the world of government and enters the digital age. It needs to be liberated from the control of a politically appointed central bank and returned to the people.

Bitcoin is the most successful attempt so far to create such a currency. Silicon Valley venture capital is lining up behind it. Young people are saving in it and some are even earning salaries in it. It is subject of feature stories in every major newspaper. Websites that accept it are becoming more prominent and profitable. It is serving as a safe haven in economically unstable countries. Every day, more merchants are accepting it.

When it first appeared in 2009, people laughed and said it would go nowhere. Four years later, it is the subject of articles in all major financial publications. Transactions happen every second. Sums in the tens of millions are moved every day by individuals, and the entire market sector has a market capitalization exceeding $1 billion — a drop in the bucket as regard world finance, but far beyond what anyone believed was possible.

Most strikingly, no politician invented Bitcoin. No commission approved it. No central bank controls it. It has absolutely no political and bureaucratic vacuum. No social consensus came up with the idea. Its success or failure depends entirely on the market. It is not even owned or controlled by a single corporation. Its value is not tied to any existing currency, but rather seeks to be its own unit of account.

Bitcoin offers a path away from monetary controls. Once you move dollars into Bitcoins, the medium of exchange is released from the Fed's fetters. This has serious implications for the conduct of monetary policy. As *Time* magazine put it:

> If a future Fed chairman tries to repeat Ben Bernanke's policy of quantitative easing (effectively printing money), worried investors could start pulling their savings out of the dollar and send it streaming into the cloud so fast that the Fed would be forced to change course... Once alternative currencies are frictionlessly available on the Internet, every laptop will become its own Cayman Islands.

In short, if the promise of Bitcoin comes to fruition, we could be watching the birth of a new global currency, one that can compete with and even replace the failed experiment in government paper currency.

If it doesn't succeed, the experience of Bitcoin itself will inspire the creation of new attempts at creating digital currency units that trade on the free market, rather than depend on governments.

To properly understand Bitcoin, you must keep in mind that its purpose is not to serve as an investment vehicle. It is an entrepreneurial invention, somewhat like the steam engine, the railroad, steel, or email. It is a pure software, based on what is called cryptography (a lynchpin of Bitcoin because it allows for privacy and unique identifiers for both coins and owners).

That technology is a payment system that is evolving as a real money. Right now its most spectacular use is in transferring funds from one person to another. It is as easy as sending a text message on a phone.

That said, all technologies are introduced into society through the commercial marketplace. That means speculation will always be part of its development — just as it was with railroads. Also part of the market will be mistakes, surprises, failings, setbacks, but also progress, triumph, and ultimately greater human satisfaction.

All the while, there will be many people who see Bitcoin and all digital currencies as a get-rich-quick scheme. People will get rich while many others will lose their shirts. But who will see the bigger picture? The trend of economic history is clear. The pressure to replace government currency with a modern alternative is intensifying every day. There will be no stopping a technology whose time has come.

BACKGROUND

Bitcoin is a decentralized electronic currency conceived in 2008 by a person or group known only as "Satoshi Nakamoto." His — or their — true identity is unknown. Nakamoto introduced the idea and the code, answered questions on an Internet forum. He wrote mostly about code but he sometimes branched out into economics and politics. His ideological orientation is indisputable: he is a believer in free markets and an opponent of government paper money. His invention was motivated by those convictions. Once his invention started to gain market traction, he disappeared without a trace.

Nakamoto designed the software that manages the currency network, along with the network that supports it. Anyone can look at the underlying code. It is not "owned" by any one group or business or individual. The Bitcoin network is controlled directly by the individual owners themselves, a system known as peer-to-peer (P2P).

The motivation being its creation tapped into a sense that most close observers have of government money. Nakamoto argued that government money relies too much on people's trust of their political elites and the system that they established. It is constantly mismanaged. No one knows what the banking elites are going to do next. It is not an open system. It is inflationary. It creates booms and busts. To top it off, it is expensive.

In contrast to the majority of other currencies, the functioning of Bitcoin is not dependent on a centralized institution. Anyone can start an exchange, retail shop, or website that tracks prices and exchanges. All of these draw from a database that is publicly distributed. The software designed by Nakamoto uses cryptography to provide security, such as the guarantee that Bitcoins may only be spent by their owner, and never more than once.

Bitcoin is one of the first implementations of the concept of crypto-currency, and without a doubt the most successful to date. Nakamoto's major achievement is the solution of the problem of double-spending in a decentralized system, which had been a major cause for concern for economists and programmers alike.

Even in the mid-1990s, programmers were talking about the need for a digital currency, but each attempt faltered because there was no way to prevent the unit from being copied — that is, to prevent fraud.

The Internet specializes in making copies. But in the area of money, copies are the kiss of death. It leads to inflation and instability and finally destroys the value of all existing currency. What we need is a money stock that is fully transparent and predictably fixed at some point in time.

Bitcoin was the first successful attempt to control copying. To prevent a Bitcoin or any fraction of a Bitcoin from being spent more than once by the same person (in other words, to avoid fraud), the network uses what Nakamoto describes as a distributed time-stamp server, which identifies and sequentially orders the transactions. Every Bitcoin is assigned an owner. This prevents their modification. The history of all Bitcoin movements remains stored in what's called the blockchain, a database that maintains a record of all transactions in the network. This information is stored in "nodes," which are nothing more than computers executing the Bitcoin software worldwide, connected to each other via the Internet. In other words, if you use Bitcoin, you are a node.

Even though Bitcoins are sent instantly and any operation may be monitored in real-time, the individual transactions are shown on screen when using the Bitcoin software that chronicles the clearing process. Worldwide, there are between 25–50 million Bitcoin transactions taking place per day. That is small compared with government currencies, but not insubstantial. You can watch Bitcoin transactions in real-time at blockchain. info. For a fun site on which to listen to music made of Bitcoin transactions, see ListentoBitcoin.com.

These exchanges are confirmed and verified by the software. The greater the number of confirmations, the more remote is the possibility of being a victim of double-spending. When a transaction exceeds six confirmations by the network, a transaction is considered technically irreversible.

How reliable is it?

To date, there is not a single documented instance of double-spending in Bitcoin. It is possible for a computer attack to hit a particular exchange, but the system as a whole cannot be hacked. So far, no one has seen a way for it to be possible for more Bitcoins to be assigned to more owners.

As a payment system that transfers funds from one person to another, it is extremely efficient. The payment is logged by the software before the network verifies that it is real and sound and then confirms the transaction. The majority of receivers and retailers who accept Bitcoins are satisfied with one single confirmation. For small amounts, it's even reasonable to accept transactions instantly, even before they are confirmed by the network.

The information that allows users to control Bitcoins in their possession can be stored in any electronic medium, such as personal hard drive, memory cards and sticks, CD, Web mailbox, etc., or in websites that offer "Bitcoin accounts."

You can keep this information on printed paper. You can even carry around such pieces of paper and use them for tipping the wait staff at a restaurant, for example. You can even keep it in your mental memory. Bitcoin ownership can be transferred through the Internet to anyone with a "Bitcoin address," similar to the way an email is sent to an email address.

Thanks to Bitcoin's cryptographic architecture, a transfer between Bitcoin addresses is far more secure than a transfer between bank accounts (and that's not counting the risk implied by the mandatory third-party intrusion within the banking system).

As it develops, we will continue to see wild swings in the price as irrational exuberance gives way to despair and back again. Bitcoin has so far proven solid as a rock. The software infrastructure built around Bitcoin will grow, fail, develop, grow, and fail again. This will happen for a long time, just as it did with email, Web media, and cellphones.

Also, as is common in these cases, some people will write it off as a failed experiment on the first dip. This has already happened in the history of Bitcoin. In 2011, the price collapsed from $30 down to $2. Even technical publications wrote it off as a failed experiment. Then it went through a revival, shooting up astronomically until the existing Bitcoin exchanges couldn't handle the load. That led to panic selling again. This could happen many more times before the market completely shakes itself out.

Remember that Bitcoin does not trade at a fixed relationship to any other currency. It is designed to be a floating currency that competes with all others. For that reason, its value will be forever fluctuating. This feature is what alarms many potential users. It acts like a wild stock and no one has any solid basis for understanding its current and potential valuation. That said, plenty of venture capitalists and many large investors are already deeply involved in the Bitcoin market.

Here is a complete picture from July 2010 to the present (April 11, 2013). You can see the wild run-up, but then a settling down at an exchange ratio of eight times its price on Jan. 1, 2013. It's been a rocky road, but the overall increase of 800% is a phenomenal increase.

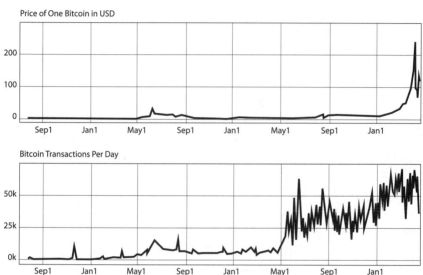

Such swings in a new market are to be expected. The first run-up and dip of Bitcoin happened as more retail outlets came online and silver fell in price. The huge run-up from $15 to $266 occurred in the midst of the Cyprus crisis and bailout. We can probably expect another upward sweep during the next currency crisis, wherever it happens to be, followed by yet another sell-off. So far, each run up and down and resulted in a new stable zone higher than it was previously.

These are the convulsions of a new currency being born. Free markets are always in a state of flux, with buyers and sellers forever participating in the process of price discovery. This is particularly true in nascent frontier markets, where early adopters meet with future waves of market participants, each with their own unique set of desires and expectations. Bitcoin has been called the "Wild Wild West" of the currency world, so it is not surprising that we should see violent swings in its price and disruptive innovations in the infrastructure serving the economy.

Left alone, markets undergo the process of "creative destruction" at breakneck pace… and they are all the better for it.

The short price history is that Bitcoin languished for most of its three-year history until it suddenly took off in March 2013, mostly in conjunction with the banking crisis in Cyprus. It shot up and fell back, but still remains at a very high point relative to its history. These gyrations have confused many people. What is the correct dollar-to-Bitcoin exchange ratio? No one knows for sure right now, just as no one knows the correct dollar-to-euro or euro-to yen exchange ratio. This is for the market — and the buyers and sellers involved therein — to decide.

IS IT MONEY?

People who use Bitcoin everyday treat it like money. Those who have no familiarity with it dismiss it entirely. Other commentators like Paul Krugman agitate against it on grounds that nothing can be money unless it is "legal tender" and controlled by a central bank.

It is true that the "peer to peer" nature of the Bitcoin network makes it impossible to establish a centralized control of the whole system. This prevents the arbitrary increase of the quantity of coins in circulation (which would cause inflation) and any other type of manipulation of their value on the part of the authorities.

The Bitcoin software (also known as "Bitcoin client") installed in users' computers transmits each transaction to nearby nodes, which in turn propagate it throughout the network. Invalid transactions are refused by honest clients (those who comply with the protocol). As yet, most transactions may be carried out free of charge, but it is possible to pay a transaction fee so that miners prioritize (speed up) their processing.

Where do new Bitcoins come from? They are "mined" the same way that gold is mined. This mining takes place when a computer works to verify transactions by solving complicated math problems. In the early days, the mining was easy. But the program is designed to make mining harder as more computers get involved in the process.

The idea here is to strictly restrain money creation. Every 10 minutes, a new block is added to the overall blockchain. Currently, each new block contains 25 additional Bitcoins. Every time 210,000 Bitcoins are mined, the production rate is halved. But just as there is only so much gold in the world, there are only so many Bitcoins.

In 2140, the total number of Bitcoins in circulation will reach 21 million. Their supply grows as a geometric series (at a constant rate). Already, more than half the total supply has generated. In 2017, three-quarters of the total supply will already be in circulation.

Bitcoins are divisible down to eight decimal points, and potentially more, which removes the practical limitations to price adjustment. In other words, one Bitcoin can buy you a cab ride or it could buy you a condominium in Manhattan, depending on the market valuation. If the value of Bitcoin rises that much, it is easy to denominate goods and services in ever smaller decimal units. If Bitcoin matures enough, its value will become independent of any existing monetary unit.

As of this writing, Bitcoin has a $1 billion-plus market capitalization. Still, the Bitcoin economy is tiny compared with well-established economies. Even so, all types of goods and services are currently being exchanged for Bitcoins, and there are many websites offering the exchange of almost every currency for Bitcoins through different funds transfer systems.

We aren't ready to say that Bitcoin is already money, though clearly many people (perhaps half a million or so) already regard it as such. But for it to be a universal money, there would have to be more general interest in its value independent of other currencies, and pricing would need to take place not based on the exchange rate, but on its own. That said, we are watching its moneyness emerge slowly, but steadily, exactly as gold and silver emerged in the past.

WHY BITCOIN IS HARD TO UNDERSTAND

Even the most qualified people have trouble understanding how Bitcoin works, just as it might have been difficult to explain email 20 years ago. The reason for this is that Bitcoin challenges a series of concepts that have rarely ever been questioned before. We need to unlearn these suppositions before adopting better ones.

Even knowing that Bitcoin is superior to any other monetary system, many people tend to prefer that with which they are familiar, rather than venturing into unknown territory. The eternal battle between the conservative — who supports the theory of "better the evil you already know" — and the adventurer — who would rather go for the "good that is yet to be known" — takes place within all of us.

But once the legacy of misconceptions has been rejected and the inertia of habit has been overcome, the path becomes far easier for the adventurer, who will also pave the way for the conservative. What are the ingrained habits that make Bitcoin appear implausible?

- We are used to seeing the act of paying as separate from the act of recording the payment. Through Bitcoin, nobody pays (nobody sends or receives Bitcoins); instead people modify balances in a sort of decentralized ledger (which is sort of like a big book). Thus, the act of paying is indistinguishable from the act of recording the payment;
- We are used to thinking that the monetary system needs to be guarded by a privileged caste of central bankers and regulators. The Bitcoin protocol does not protect someone or some group in particular, but rather protects the tool itself and, therefore, all those who use it;
- We are used to our bank accounts being linked to our identity. Bitcoin addresses are anonymous if their owners so wish;
- We are used to transactions that are known in detail only by those directly involved in them (plus the third-party payment processor). With Bitcoin, information about all transactions is public and easily accessible;
- We are used to money as a receipt with more or less backing. With Bitcoin, the unit and the receipt are the same "thing," and impossible to duplicate or to falsify.

WILL THERE BE A CRACKDOWN?

One possible failure scenario for Bitcoin is that of a worldwide governmental campaign against the software and the sites that accept Bitcoins. The Financial Crimes Enforcement Network has already intervened to insist that miners and exchanges register the same way any currency trader does. The FBI is carefully watching Bitcoin for fear that it is a vehicle for money laundering. Other government agencies will certainly get involved, wanting to regulate and control.

What about the ultimate fear that government will simply outlaw digital currency? Given the nature of the system, the total elimination of Bitcoin (as that of any other P2P network) does not seem either technologically or economically viable. It is just not possible to rid the world of particular combinations of 1s and 0s. Government is powerful, but not that powerful. Even if something called "Bitcoin" were made illegal, the currency could be reinvented under another name.

There are certain factors mitigating against even the attempt. Large corporations are already accepting it. Venture capital has already put vast sums into development. It is a global, not a national, currency, meaning the difficulties of unified laws and enforcement are vastly more.

There's an additional factor here too. Bitcoin is the greatest tool ever invented for passing money from one party to another without a paper trail. This is something that politicians, bureaucrats, and government employees of all sorts in all lands desire very intensely — even more than regular citizens. It might remain untouched for that reason alone.

Nobody knows for certain what Bitcoin's destiny will be; the only thing we know is that the idea of a decentralized crypto-currency is here to stay.

THE TECHNICAL SUPERIORITY OF BITCOIN

Why is Bitcoin superior to government currencies? The quick answer: Because no one — no committee of "experts" — controls its destiny and because the rules set by the protocol devised by Satoshi Nakamoto are not imposed; each user chooses to accept them. Like a free society, Bitcoin manages itself. But what does this mean in practice for the user?

Let's list the advantages. Bitcoin:

- Strengthens privacy by eliminating the interference of third parties in transactions.
- Increases in supply at a predictable and slowing rate, helping to preserve — and possibly even increase — Bitcoin's purchasing power.
- Lowers, or even eliminates, transaction costs on the Web. Fees and costs associated with current methods of exchange —Visa, MasterCard, and even PayPal — tend to hinder free exchange.
- Simplifies and accelerates payments, dispensing with unwanted intermediaries.
- Affords users anonymity, if they desire it.
- Allows transfers anywhere, ignoring geographic and political barriers.

- Fosters transparency: Although users are not forced to reveal their identities, all transactions are recorded in a freely accessible record so that errors can be spotted quickly.
- Supports complex transactions (escrow, deposit insurance, guarantees, mediation, etc.) with solid cryptographic support for all types of rules and conditions that are freely agreed upon by the parties.
- Is available nonstop: There are no holidays or weekends for Bitcoin operations.
- Makes micropayments viable on a large scale.
- Prevents the freezing of funds.
- Prevents chargebacks.
- Prevents the arbitrary restriction of goods and services that may be purchased.
- Allows for the accumulation of huge fortunes within a very tiny space.
- Can be easily hidden and does not need to resort to a third party for safekeeping and/ or transfer.
- Can be stored in multiple locations simultaneously.
- Does not rely on a third party or a particular legal system to preserve its value.
- Provides protection against all forms of theft, including taxes: The technology on which the Bitcoin protocol is based is several times safer than that used by banks and credit cards.
- Cannot be removed by legal/computer attacks, due to its decentralized nature.
- Cannot be forged.
- Is easily and instantly recognizable.
- Is infinitely divisible.

For quite a few reasons that no one any longer denies, email has replaced the postal service in all its primary duties. How many reasons in its favor does Bitcoin have to build up for fiat money to become obsolete? It could be rocky road forward, but there will be no letup in the pressure for the world to embrace precisely what Bitcoin represents.

OK, I'M IN. WHAT SHOULD I DO TO GET STARTED?

Now that you've seen the advantages, you might be ready to jump in. But before you do, remember that this market is far from being settled, and your own technical skill needs time to develop. It is best to start very small, just to get a feel for it. People who first enter this sector can sometimes make mistakes that result in lost coins. Even today's experts will tell you that "user error" has resulted in problems in the past. Start small; you can ramp up your holdings later on.

In addition, the Bitcoin industry is completely open and it will likely attract a sizable number of crooks and scam artists. For this reason, you should use only reputable sites. New companies will come along and proclaim themselves to be wonderful. Modern website design can make anything seem wonderful.

But here is a truth you must remember: All exchanges and websites are subject to crashing and hacking. With healthy competition, this will happen less and less over time. But in the intervening period, you should keep possession of your own Bitcoins and not trust an institution that claims to be a bank to keep them for you. One of the great advantages of Bitcoin is precisely that you do not need banks.

If, while you are exploring an option, anything strikes you as odd, if you see any strange pop-up advertising, if there is the slightest sign of trouble, back away. There are other places to go. Another glory of Bitcoin is that it allows you to move money almost instantly and with no fuss from one vendor to another and back again.

HOW TO GET STARTED: YOUR BITCOIN WALLET

The first step in getting Bitcoins into your possession so that you can trade with them is to obtain a "wallet." The Bitcoin wallet is the file needed to send and receive Bitcoins. This file contains our Bitcoins, although in reality, it contains cryptographic keys (unique, secret, private keys) that make us owners of our Bitcoins and allow us to authorize payments (transfer the possession of our coins). The word *wallet* actually applies, however. It is the piece of equipment that keeps track of your Bitcoins and allows you to use them.

Getting one or more wallets is easy; here are the two most popular ways of doing it:

The Official Way

Bitcoin-Qt (the name of the official Bitcoin client) is a program that can be installed on any computer that runs Windows, Mac or Linux. You just need to download it from Bitcoin.org and install it. It will automatically create a wallet and will start downloading the transaction history (blockchain). You need only be online to send from this wallet; it's not necessary to be online if you just want to receive Bitcoins. This method is used by the most technically sophisticated among users. Once you have this wallet, you can then sign up with an exchange. Two examples are Mt. Gox and the newer American exchange called Tradehill. Both are reputable and tested by users. More are on their way.

The Easy Way

In the old days of only two years ago, users had to have a high degree of technical expertise to use Bitcoin. Now there's a new generation of Web wallets that are very safe and easy to use. Their level of security relies on the fact that the private keys are encrypted in the user's browser, so the service provider will never have access to your Bitcoins.

The two best and most reputable wallets are available from Coinbase. com and Blockchain.info. These companies both offer free smartphone applications.

You should begin by downloading the smartphone application. Whatever you download to your smartphone you can (and should) duplicate on your desktop computer. That way, you have two ways to access your Bitcoin wallet.

The one we recommend is My Wallet, offered by Blockchain. If you don't want to go through the entire tutorial, simply do the following:

Download the Blockchain app on your device. Register with a 10- digit password. And that's it. Now you are ready to receive Bitcoins.

The detailed tutorial below describes the process using My Wallet from Blockchain.info. This is a tutorial for using the website edition, although the smartphone edition is the same. Again, we recommend doing both to ensure you have two ways to access your wallet.

Again, this is to date the easiest and most secure method.

SETTING UP YOUR BITCOIN WALLET – TUTORIAL

Go to Blockchain.info/wallet. Click on the "Start a New Wallet" button.

Fill in your alias and a password of your choice, and copy the CAPTCHA.

Regarding the password: Use at least 10 characters, do not include any words or names, and try to use uppercase letters, lowercase letters, numbers, and (ideally) other symbols. Try not to use "regular" words, because there are robots on the Web that use what are called "dictionary attacks" to rapidly try out passwords and attempt to guess yours.

For example, your password should not be johnsmith1. It should be more like j0hn5mi1h#. This is very important not only in signing up for Bitcoin, but for all your online dealings.

Whatever you do, don't forget your password. You cannot recover it.

Create A New Wallet.

Please choose an alias and password for the new wallet.

Email: _____

(Optional) - We will email you a link to your new wallet.

Password: _____

Confirm Password: _____

Captcha: _____

Continue

The next screen will present you with a mnemonic that you can use to retrieve your password in the future, in case you forget it. Make sure you write it down and make some copies.

It is important that you don't lose your password. If you do, you will lose your Bitcoins

(Blockchain.info does not save this information).

Wallet Recovery Mnemonic

Your wallet has been created successfully. If you forget the details the phrase below can be used to recover everything.

Please Write Down the Following:

Do not save the mnemonic on your PC or in your email drafts! Write it down or print it!

Without the mnemonic we cannot help recover forgotten passwords and will result in **LOSS of ALL of your bitcoins!**.

Print   Continue

The next screen you'll see will be the login page to your wallet. The URL should read

https://blockchain.info/wallet/YourAlias. You will see two boxes: one for your wallet's identifier (a long string of characters, such as 0d683d57-b040-3d0c-f43e-0a83d15b0aef) and one for your password.

Enter the password you selected in Step 3 and you'll be taken to your wallet.

Blockchain   Home Charts Stats Markets

My Wallet Be Your Own Bank.

Wallet Home   My Transactions   Send Money   Receive Money   Import / Export

Welcome Back
Please enter your login details below:

Identifier:

Password:

Open Wallet

Congratulations! You're now inside your wallet.

Next, you can go to your account settings, where you'll have access to your account information. In reality, there's no need to change any of the settings. Your wallet is good to go as it stands, with one exception.

Back up Your Wallet

You'll want an easy way to back up your wallet (something you should ALWAYS do). There are two ways to do this, with your email address or directly from your wallet.

Backing up Your Wallet via Your Email Address

Do this by entering your email address in the space where it is requested. This will send a confirmation code, which you will need to enter in the "confirmation code box" below where you entered your email.

Account Settings Change your My Wallet account settings.

ACCOUNT INFORMATION

- Personal
- General
- Display
- Notifications
- Passwords
- Security

Email (Recommended)

An email is needed to help recover a lost wallet identifier and for payment notifications.

Your Email

Email Verification Code:

Email Verification Code   Verify   Resend Link

As soon as your email address is verified, you will receive your wallet's backup in your inbox. If you save your email, you are fine. If not, save this file somewhere safe and/or store it in the cloud. Even if the website (blockchain.info) disappears, you'll have access to your Bitcoins with this backup file.

Backing up Your Wallet via Your Wallet Home (if you don't want to use your email address):

Go to "Wallet Home." And at the bottom right, you'll see a "Backup" area with some buttons for downloading your wallet's backup. The "Download" button will allow you to save the backup file directly into your computer; the "Dropbox" button will connect to your Dropbox account to save the file there; same thing with the "Google Drive" button. The "Email" button is just another way to do what we described above.

Receiving Bitcoins:

Now this is the fun part. You have your wallet set up. Now you can actually receive Bitcoins. You can do this in one of two ways: Either you buy them from an exchange for paper money or someone gives them to you for trade.

The easiest possible way is to find someone you know who uses them. Most anyone is happy to give away 0.001 Bitcoin just to get a new convert involved. This person will know all about scanning QR codes from phone to phone. This is the fastest and easiest way.

Anytime you are receiving Bitcoins, you need to use your Bitcoin address (the same information is stored in your QR code). In your wallet's Home, you'll see your Bitcoin address at the bottom left. It'll look something like this: 1BFyhVVBVG8EuK3Upv738Bqd7e8hmGmgxu.

This is the address you need to give to the person who's going to send you the coins (make sure you copy and paste it to avoid mistakes). You can create more addresses, which will all point to your wallet. It is very useful to have different addresses to organize your wallet. So you could have an address for your business, another for Bitcoin purchases, etc.

This is how you create them:

Go to "Receive Money."

You'll see your default address listed there (the same that showed on the wallet's Home). Go to the bottom right corner and click on the "New Address" button.

A new window will pop up with a new generated address. Here you'll be able to label your address as you wish (i.e., Business).

Your new address will show on the list. So next time you need to receive coins from a business-related transaction, you will be able to use this address and keep payments separated (you can create as many addresses as you want).

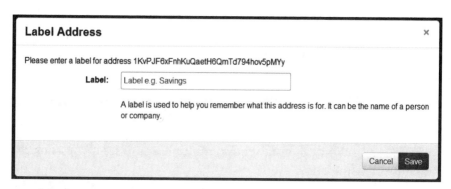

Sending Bitcoins:

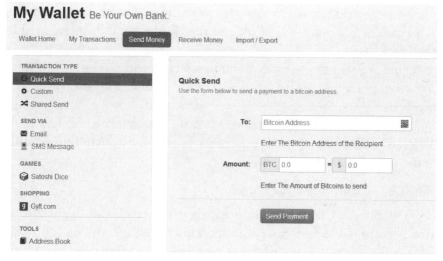

From your wallet's Home, go to "Send Money."

From here you can do a "Quick" send or a "Custom" send. If you just want to send some coins and you don't mind from which address they're going to be deducted, just use the quick option. Now, if you're sending coins related to your business activity, you might want to deduct the amount from the "Business" address you created. For this, you need to use the Custom send (just click on "Custom" at the left, under the Transaction Type dashboard).

Let's say you selected the Custom send. The first thing you'll need to do is select the address you'll be deducting your coins from (in our case, we'll select "Business" from the menu).

In the "To" box, you'll need to enter the address of the person you're sending the Bitcoins to (make sure to copy and paste the address

To:	Bitcoin Address		BTC	0.0	$ 0.00
	Bitcoin Address		BTC	0.0	$ 0.00
	Bitcoin Address		BTC	0.0	$ 0.00

Total Value: 0 (Available: 0.00 BTC)

to avoid errors). You can even send to multiple addresses if you click the "+" button to the right.

Next to the address, you'll need to enter the Bitcoin amount you are sending (i.e., 1.45BTC).

You can add a note to the transaction if you want. But be careful what you say: Anyone will be able to read it, since it'll be embedded in the blockchain.

There's also a drop-down menu to select to which address you want the change to be directed. Select the same one you are taking the funds from.

Hit "Review Payment" and confirm it if the information is correct. You can access a history of all your transactions going to "My Transactions" at the top of your wallet's Home.

How Does a Bitcoin Wallet Work?

The Bitcoin Client will automatically generate a wallet that will contain a pair of public and (their corresponding) private keys. This is the way encryption works. For the purposes of the user, you only need to be concerned with your public key. The public keys are the ones you can see — the ones you give to the other party when you want to receive a payment. Private keys, however, are stored in your wallet (in the wallet.dat file).

Imagine your public addresses as being inviolable mailboxes that everyone can see and in which anyone can deposit their Bitcoins. Each public key is "opened" with a specific, impossible-to-duplicate private key that is stored on your software.

If you receive 1 Bitcoin, it has been sent to one of your public keys (or address). The only way to transfer the ownership of that Bitcoin (to "send" it to another person) is by using the stored private key that corresponds to that public address.

As long as you keep the wallet, you'll possess the private keys that will allow you to use the Bitcoins controlled by that wallet. That's why it's a good idea to keep backups.

Once you have your Bitcoin wallet, there are several ways you can get more Bitcoins.

Exchanges and Trading Sites:

There are many sites where you can get small fractions of Bitcoins for free. These sites are filled with advertisements and can be tricky to use. They might be fun to play with, and there's nothing wrong with doing that, but they are not for people who are truly interested in using or saving Bitcoins.

You can also deal with a local dealer and trade cash for Bitcoins at a premium.

What you really need to do is sign up for an account with a real Bitcoin exchange. This requires linking your bank account the same way you would do electronic banking with a utility company, your cable company, or your credit card company. The steps you go through are the same. Think of the Bitcoin exchange as just another vendor you deal with.

The most known and used Bitcoin exchange to date is Mt. Gox. It handles 80% of all Bitcoin trade.

But there are many other sites that facilitate the exchange with all types of currencies and that support various systems for transferring funds. BitInstant, Bitstamp, Bitcoin Nordic, Coinbase, and mercaBit are just some that sell Bitcoins through hundreds of thousands of points of sale worldwide.

Of all these, Coinbase is the most popular because it easiest. Your bank will probably refuse Coinbase's attempt to connect until the account is verified. This happens in the usual way: Two small deposits will be made into your account. When they arrive, you put those amounts into Coinbase, and then you are linked up.

A new American exchange that is working hard to make Bitcoin more mainstream is Tradehill. All of the main exchanges today require a great deal of identity checking. You will face a double confirmation that you are, indeed, the owner of the bank account you link. For those who think of Bitcoin as a way to disappear financially, this process will show otherwise. All of these exchanges work very hard to legitimize their businesses.

In addition, there are sites that accept payments through Western Union or Liberty Reserve, like Nanaimo Gold. There are sites that accept gold and silver in exchange for Bitcoins (and vice versa), like Coinabul.

Please note: You can make new wallets and new accounts all you want. If you have a blockchain wallet and a Coinbase.com desktop and want to move the money, you can send from one to the other and back again — all without notable fees. This is vastly easier than making a regular account.

Accepting Bitcoins for goods and services:

Do you have a business for which you are interested in accepting Bitcoins? There are many services out there that will help you set up an e-commerce solution to y our business. Coinbase does this. But the most popular is BitPay.com

There are tens of thousands of vendors that accept Bitcoins, and the invaluable Bitcoin Wiki is updated by the minute to tell you who they are. For example, you can buy supplies for your business from Amazon with BTC4amazon. Or you can buy from the "Amazon" of Bitcoin itself: BitcoinStore.com.

Through them, you can:

- buy gift and debit cards (CryptCard, BTCinstant)
- buy precious metals (Amagi Metals)
- buy novelty physical Bitcoins (CoinedBits)
- trade equities (MPEx)
- buy gold and crude futures (ICBIT)
- get a website designed (FarmGeek)
- order flowers (BitcoinForFlowers)
- buy pharmaceuticals without a prescription and at half price (JCM Pharmacy)
- buy electronics and books (Bitcoinin)
- post classifieds (BitcoinClassifieds)
- buy survival food and storage (Survival Food)
- go to photography school (Icon Photography)
- buy beauty products (Bitcoin Knotwork)
- donate to charity (BitCharity)
- and thousands of other things…

This is only a tiny sample. Again, Bitcoin Wiki is updated daily with information on where you can use your Bitcoins.

However, one of the most popular services in the Bitcoin world right now, sometimes credited with having made paying with Bitcoin mainstream, is Bitspend.net. Here you can put in any Web address from a commercial site and pay with Bitcoins, instead of dollars. This

site is so popular that it crashed in its first week. Now it is stable and a wonderful way to use Bitcoins at any store you want.

Contrary to popular opinion, the retail and wholesale Bitcoin sector is actually better developed than the exchange sector. It is possible to set a price in any currency and denominate it in Bitcoin automatically at current exchange rates so that the cost won't be affected by fluctuations.

Through BitPay, payments can also be automatically converted to the currency the merchant prefers. (So your customers can pay with Bitcoin, but you will receive dollars, if that's your choice. Many of the merchants accepting Bitcoin now are us-ing this. Examples include WordPress, OkCupid, and Reddit. Namecheap is an-other good example of a company that is providing this.)

If you are interested in following just the dollar/Bitcoin exchange rate, there are innumerable apps you can download for free on your cellphone. They display prices like this:

FINDING PEOPLE WILLING TO SELL THEIR BITCOINS:

You can locate people who want to sell by using services such as TradeBitcoin, LocalBitcoins, or specialized forums, among other places. There are many miners who sell their produce and local traders who buy and sell for a commission. It is very common for people to get together at some neutral location, such as a Wi-Fi cafe or restaurant.

If you have a friend who has a Bitcoin wallet, it is easy to move Bitcoins back and forth. You can get their Bitcoin address (they can email it or text it) and send Bitcoins that way with the push of a button.

Another way to send someone Bitcoins is by scanning their QR code (the square design that looks like a block barcode). It looks like a version of this:

Scanning this code puts their identifier in your send address. In the blank that allows you to specify the amount you want to send, be careful to put in the right amount. You might start with trying to send only a tiny amount, such as 0.001BTC.

If you are on the receiving end of the transaction, you need only hold up your code and ask your friend to scan it.

Once you trade with someone, you will be asked if you want to add this person to your address book, thereby replacing the long alphanumeric code with a simple name. This is a very good idea. That way you can have it for later dealings. You don't need to scan again.

You should be fastidious about putting this information in your wallet. That way, you do not risk accidentally sending money to someone you did not intend to. All transactions clear in as little as a few seconds to as long as a few minutes. These wallets are all in an early version of the software. As such, they are subject to human error. If you make a mistake, it cannot be undone. Such is the fate of every first generation of software.

MINING

Once upon a time, many people made lots of money mining Bitcoins. But due to the increased difficulty of obtaining Bitcoins through this means (related to the ever-increasing computational power being added by miners to the Bitcoin's network), nowadays, it is essential to have 1) a very high computational power and 2) use a mining pool to be able to have shared results.

It's been a long time since mining ceased to be within reach of the average PC user, and even the most powerful servers are being left behind by a superpowerful card called ASIC. More and more, mining is being left to specialists. *At this late stage, mining is not profitable for average users.* It will cost you more in equipment than you will earn.

BANKS, FAILURES, AND COLD STORAGE

With fiat money, we are used to fearing bank runs that come in wake of financial problems and bankruptcy. Even with deposit insurance, people worry that they won't get their money back. With Bitcoin, those fears largely evaporate, because every Bitcoin or fraction of a Bitcoin has an owner, and that owner directly controls its fate. There is no need for traditional banking in the way we've come to think about it.

Consider the case in April of the shutting down of a major Bitcoin exchange called BitFloor.com. It's account with its bank was closed for reasons no one yet knows. It put a sign on its website saying that it had stopped business. Many of its customers were very upset, but why? Because of the inconvenience. But the fear that the money would somehow not be there for all customers was nowhere in sight. The Bitcoin exchange rate was completely unaffected. It barely made the news.

The Bitcoin sector has given rise to certain kinds of warehousing functions. You can put your Bitcoins in what is called "cold storage." Let's say you own a large amount, say, 1,000 Bitcoin. You do not need instant access to them. In fact, you'd feel better if you did not. You can use any of the main services to put those in cold storage for safekeeping. You can even download your Bitcoins and keep your own cold storage on a thumb drive. You can even print out your Bitcoins and keep them in a safe place. Then, when you need them, you can transfer them back into online use.

How can you be sure that a company that is keeping your Bitcoins in cold storage will not use them for some other purpose? Every Bitcoin and every fraction of a Bitcoin has a unique identifier. The transactions that take place are all posted publicly on the blockchain. If they were ever moved, you would know instantly, and a permanent digital trail would exist. For this reason, it would be extremely difficult, if not impossible, to steal any Bitcoin without the owner's knowledge.

SOME FINAL DISTINCTIONS

The glory of the market economy is its instability. Perhaps that sounds strange to stay, but the truth is that a perfectly stable market is one where there is no growth, no advance, and no progress. There is only stasis. That is precisely the way governments like the world to work, because it allows them to control it, which means controlling you.

Markets thwart that desire completely. There are new ideas, new products, new technologies, new services, and new ways of doing business. This is essential. But this process is always trial and error. Nothing is perfect out of the gate. Enterprise is in a great position to learn from these mistakes, but the mistakes have to happen in order to provide that lesson.

In the future, we are likely to see the development of Bitcoin deposit insurance, more robust futures markets, insurance markets, instant micropayments for online services, a broad-based debit card market, a BTC-denominated stock market, and so much more. We are still in the infancy of this technology, which could not only create a new global economic sector, but could actually end up redefining the relationship between the individual and the state.

In the early days of the Internet, the technology was new and the providers were not prepared for its rapid growth. On the consumer end, of course, everyone expected everything to work perfectly. Speculators got involved, and the usual hysteria and the madness of crowds took over. At the first sign of trouble, overbought stocks crashed, people bailed, sentiment changed, and many people declared the new system dead.

Of course, the Internet did not die. It has been a source of economic growth for the last 15 years and it will continue this way. Those who placed their trust in the conventional wisdom — this new system can never work — ended up on the wrong side of history.

That same cycle seems to be repeating itself with Bitcoin. For the first two years of its existence, it languished at 14 cents to the dollar. Then, as its merits were discovered and retailers got involved, the software infrastructure could not handle the increased load. It became overbought, and panic selling ensued. All over social media and among those who doubt there is any merit to Bitcoin at all, there was widespread chortling and declarations that Bitcoin failed.

But these pronouncements missed a crucial distinction. There is a huge difference between Bitcoin as a technology and Bitcoin exchanges as institutions. Every single Bitcoin exchange could fail, but that says nothing about the success or failure of Bitcoin as a technology. It's like declaring railroads a failure because the train didn't arrive on time, or judging email to be bad because the earliest services were spotty.

Think back to the Pets.com fiasco of 2000. Just because this one company flopped did not mean that Internet commerce was dead. On the contrary, the death of this institution and many others taught lessons for others to follow.

So it is with Bitcoin.

Right now, 67% of Bitcoin trades go through Mt. Gox. If this company has technical trouble, the entire market is affected. This is a frustrating fact for many people in the whole industry. People are calling for more exchanges and a greater diversification of holding, and there will be more. There will be thousands of exchanges in the future.

The exchange rate crash from a high of $266 to a low of $50 in the course of 48 hours was linked to the failure of Mt. Gox, which had servers that became wildly overloaded. It didn't help being hit with distributed denial-of-service (DDoS) attacks at the same time. Such attacks usually originate from robots sending rapid-fire submissions through data-receiving portions of the website. Such attacks afflict every website in the course of its life, and they can only be prevented once they have occurred, allowing network administrators to customize the server against the most likely attacks.

But the DDoS hammerings of Mt. Gox in early April exacerbated panic selling and the dramatic price drop. So frustrated were the server's managers that they actually suspended trading for 12 hours, leaving only a handful of other exchanges and a very thin market.

This was not the first such case, and it won't be the last. Mt. Gox has already dramatically improved its server infrastructure since this event. But still, the faults of one exchange should not affect an entire industry so dramatically, which is why so many people are working toward diversification.

As Matt Ridley has written:

> It would be a mistake to write off Bitcoins as just another bubble. People are clearlykeen on new forms of money safe from the confiscation and inflation that looks increasingly inevitable as governments try to escape their debts. Bitcoins pose a fundamental question: Will some form of private money replace the kind minted and printed by governments?

Even if Bitcoin does achieve that end, wild swings will continue to be part of this industry. This is why so many people are looking forward to new innovations, including Bitcoin ATMs. I actually used one of the prototypes while at a New Hampshire conference. They are currently being perfected for release in the coming months. Innovators are already looking at plugins for existing ATMs that will allow quick conversions. When this happens, people will be in a position to move in and out quickly.

Just keep this in mind: Bitcoins are not conceived of as an investment vehicle. Until the market stabilizes and until you become technically adept at using them, you should never keep more money in Bitcoins than you can afford to lose. Some people have made, and will continue to make, a killing on speculation. But you can't (and shouldn't) count on being among them. The exchange rate could take years to stabilize. During this period, it will respond to unpredictable events, such as bank failures.

Even if the long-run pressure is for Bitcoin to become more valuable in terms of goods and services, we are likely to see more downward swoops as well.

On the other hand, venture capital is all over this market. As TechCrunch says:

> Bitcoin's record highs and the ensuring surge in hacking attempts and thefts may be grabbing headlines. However, beneath the chaos, Silicon Valley's best-known venture firms are finally starting to make real bets around the crypto-currency.
>
> The price of a single Bitcoin had more than quintupled to $265 amid a banking crisis in Cyprus and new signs from the U.S. Treasury's Financial Crimes Enforcement Network that regulators will tolerate the currency. It then settled back down to $120 as increased volumes and DDoS attacks hit the biggest Bitcoin exchanges today and yesterday. While anyone who has ever worked in trading knows that a chart like this often ends in a world of pain, there is a growing sense that Bitcoin, or another math-based currency like it, is here to stay."

The purpose of Bitcoin is to serve as a digital-age payment system, evolving one step at a time into an independent money to compete with that forced on us by the nation-state. It may sound like a dream, but we've already seen digital technology make many dreams come true, including instantaneous and wireless video phones that are free and allow you to speak with anyone in the world.

The best way forward for you as an individual is to become an owner. If anything in this report confused you, or it all seemed a bit abstract, owning is the true remedy. That's what changes everything. If it is at tiny amount like 0.0001 BTC, owning is the key to l earning and then doing.

Markets are continually reinventing the world. Might they do the same thing for money? And banking? And insurance? And financial services? It is a trial-and-error process, but many people are dedicated to making it happen. Between now and then, it will be a wild and wonderful ride. We do, indeed, live in interesting times.

6 TAKING BACK YOUR FINANCIAL FREEDOM

Don't put your financial future in the hands of Washington politicians and Wall Street brokers. Put yourself back in the driver seat with some of these helpful suggestions.

IS COLLEGE REALLY WORTH IT? YOU DECIDE.

It used to be that part of the American dream was getting your kids ready for college. They needed to earn a degree that would then allow them to get a successful job once they entered the workforce. But that is a dream from another time.

Now sending your kids off to college isn't as lucrative as it once was. The next largest debt in America after housing is student loan debt. On average, students are leaving college with over $20,000 of debt, making it extremely difficult to begin saving in their early employment years. After they leave college, they're entering a job market that's becoming more and more unfriendly to recent graduates.

And since student loans are one of the few types of loans that don't go away after declaring bankruptcy, these students can expect to carry this debt long after they take their last class.

Considering the circumstances surrounding college and the opportunities it creates, it's safe to ask whether sending your child or grandchild is actually a good investment. Maybe the better question would be what major and focus in college offers them the best opportunity to avoid this debt.

One report by Thomas C. Frohlich lists the top seven professions that don't require a college degree and their median salaries. Keep in

mind that the people who obtain these jobs out of college aren't saddled
with thousands of dollars of college loans that need to be repaid:

1. Subway and Streetcar Operators $62,730
2. Fashion Designers $62,860
3. Power Distributors and Dispatchers $71,690
4. Detectives and Criminal Investigators $74,300
5. Nuclear Power Reactor Operators $74,990
6. Elevator Installers and Repairers $76,650
7. Airline Pilots, Co-pilots and Flight Engineers $114,200

The last category is very interesting. Many pilots have bachelor's
degrees, but many receive their qualifications from either the military
or flight schools. In many cases, college-level classes are necessary.

High school graduates who don't go to college might be excluded
from some entry-level positions that require a college degree, but they
will still qualify for many professional positions. Also, they're not exposed
to the student loan bubble and won't be devastated if/when it finally pops.

Whether or not you decide to send your child to college, the most
important thing is that you're informed prior to making any big decisions.
More importantly, the prospective college student should know what kind
of job market he or she might face after delaying working for four years.

THE FASTEST GROWING INDUSTRIES IN AMERICA

Taking a long-term look at the economy, there are certain sectors
that offer a bright future. The highest-growth industries of the economies offer the best chance for long-term employment.

Sageworks, a financial information company, analyzed the financial
statements of various privately owned companies to see what businesses
were growing in our stagnant economy. Their results are unsurprising
when you consider the economic changes going on around the country
in 2013:

Industry	Sales Growth Last 12 Months
Support Activities for Mining	32%
Petroleum and Petroleum-Related Merchant Wholesalers	27%
Industrial Machinery Manufacturing	25%
Cattle Ranching and Farming	24%

Architectural and Structural Metals Manufacturing	23%
Metalworking Machinery Manufacturing	21%
Machine Shops, Turned Product, Bolt Manufacturing	19%
Employment Services	18%
Gasoline Stations	18%
Computer Systems Design and Related Services	18%

With all the relatively recent oil finds throughout the country, it's not surprising that the fastest-growing industries are somehow related to energy production. There's not much evidence to suggest that this trend won't continue into the future as America strives to become a net exporter of energy, making these industries some of the most successful and most stable in the economy.

MAINTAINING YOUR CREDIT SCORE

The country's finances are a mess, and every so often, the government makes a big spectacle about raising the debt ceiling to pay their expenses. Rather than address the real problem of runaway government spending, they normally come up with some compromise that kicks the can further down the road for future generations to deal with.

But just because the United States doesn't know how to manage its credit rating doesn't mean you should follow suit. It's very likely you have a better understanding of finances than the politicians that run the government. Maintaining the credit score you've worked hard to achieve isn't difficult if you keep these ideas in mind.

1. Knowledge is power. And knowing what goes into your credit score is the first thing you should do. There are five pieces of information that make up your credit score: your payment history, level of debt, credit age, mix of credit, and recent credit. Not every financial action you make, however, will affect your credit rating. So for example, if you overdraft your checking account, that won't automatically hurt your credit rating.

2. Pay your bills on time. If someone is going to loan you money, one of the most important things they like to see is that you pay your bills on time. That's why missing credit

card or loan payments can quickly drop your credit rating.
Set up online calendars that will email or text you alerts
when various payments are due so you can plan ahead and
make sure you have enough money to pay them.

3. Don't max out your credit cards. One metric that factors
   into your credit score is your debt-to-credit ratio. Imagine
   you have one credit card with a $1,000 limit. If you
   maxed out that card, your debt-to-credit ratio would be
   1 ($1,000/$1,000). If you had only put $500 on the card,
   your debt-to-credit ratio would be 0.5 ($500/$1,000).
   That ratio across your entire credit history goes into
   determining your credit score.

THREE THINGS YOU CAN DO TO IMPROVE YOUR CREDIT

If you're looking to improve your credit rating, there are some steps
you can take. It might take some time, but if you follow these ideas, you
should see your score improve over time:

1. Carefully go over your most recent score. The people who
   compile your credit history are human, and occasionally
   they make mistakes. They might have mistakenly marked
   you down for missing a credit card payment. Even that
   one missed payment can have a negative effect on your
   overall credit rating. Be sure to keep detailed records of
   any payments you make with either a hard copy backup
   or an email confirmation.

2. Setting up payment reminders not only helps you maintain
   your credit, but can also help you rebuild it. Until you get
   into a normal monthly routine of paying your credit card
   bills, you should rely on automatic reminders prompting
   you when bills are due. In fact, even after you've made it a
   part of your routine, it's a good idea to keep those reminders active. Who knows when you might get distracted by
   events in your life and forget to submit a payment. Having
   an automatic reminder acts as a fail-safe in case something
   like that occurs.

3. Reduce the amount of debt you owe. One of the best ways to do this is to start paying almost all your expenses in cash. Doing this allows you to get a better understanding of your personal cash flow and how much you need to cut back in order to pay off your bills. Take any credit cards out of your wallet so you're not tempted to use them. Finally, try to pay off the credit cards with the highest interest rates.

MELT AWAY DEBT WITH THESE SIMPLE STEPS

Helpful tips on how to pay down your debt:

1. Like many things in life, the government might actually be impeding your ability to pay off your debt. Use this tip if you want to stick it to Uncle Sam while also getting some extra cash to put toward your debt. Figure out how much money you normally owe in taxes. If your withholding is too high, you'll get that money back after you file your taxes in a refund check. Instead of waiting until the government sends you back your own money, lower your withholding to cover what you expect to owe in taxes. The extra money you receive can then be put toward lowering your credit debt.

2. Don't expect to pay off your debt by making only minimum payments. Those minimum payments might give you some financial room to breathe, but they're actually making credit cards companies boatloads of profits. Paying down your debt is going to require some big sacrifices on your part. This means putting as much toward the cards as you can. Every dollar paid above the minimum payment will save you time and money in the long run.

3. Sell your unwanted stuff. Garage sales can be great ways to generate some much needed cash to put toward your credit card bills. Look around your house and pick out three things that you can do without. The money you could possibly get for them is just sitting there waiting to be claimed. With online marketplaces like Amazon and

eBay making it easy to find potential buyers, there's no reason you can't sell some unwanted items around the house.

BECOME A "CABLE-CUTTER" AND REDUCE YOUR CABLE BILL TO ZERO

Ever since the Internet emerged, it has redefined many prominent industries in our economy. From how you listen to music to how you communicate with people overseas, the Internet broke down the old business model and replaced it with something better. Now it stands ready to do the same for how you watch TV.

If you're like many Americans, you probably watch some amount of television online. Various websites offer reruns of old episodes for free to anyone who logs on to the site. Specialty websites like Hulu emerged as places where viewers could easily find and access the shows they want. Many customers are leaving behind the old business model where TV networks feed them programming at set times on specific days. Instead, they're taking control of how they consume their television programming.

Most Americans probably pay for both cable television and Internet service. They're bundled into one bill, but both still have to be paid for. However, many "cable cutters," people who pay for only the Internet, have figured out a way to get all their standard television while lowering their cable bill to $0.

Using a traditional "bunny ear" antenna, you can receive high-definition television broadcasts from the major TV networks. In addition to that, you can buy either an Apple TV or Roku streaming device. These allow you to access many online content providers. You can connect your online Netflix account and watch streaming episodes of any shows they provide. As Netflix launches more and more original television series, the quality of content will continue to increase.

If there are television shows you normally watch on basic cable, you can purchase them for a small fee the day after. Most of the time, you spend less money buying individual episodes via Amazon or iTunes than you do paying basic cable for the entire month. On top of that, the episodes you do buy are yours to keep. You can re-watch them anytime.

DISCOUNTED HOME APPLIANCES RIGHT UNDER YOUR NOSE

If you're in the market for a home appliance, take note of the following ideas to save some money. If you've purchased electronic equipment over the Internet, you're probably aware of what refurbished and reconditioned items are. In case you don't know, they're practically brand-new products that have been returned for one reason or another.

Since they've been opened, they can't be labeled as new. But since they were hardly used, they don't have to be listed as used, either. In most cases, stores will list them as reconditioned. And because of this, they give you a discount on the price. Before you say you'd rather buy a new product than risk buying a reconditioned one, there's something you should be aware of. These open-box products normally are a better buy than new ones.

Let me explain. Every time a retailer receives a returned product, they take a financial hit. There are costs associated with reimbursing a customer as well as restocking. The last thing they want to do is put the item back up for sale only to have it returned because it doesn't work. So the retailer makes sure the product is in 100% working order before they offer it for sale.

This is a level of service not given to most new products. In many cases, it'd be impossible for an inspector to ensure that every product coming off the assembly line works perfectly. They take accurate samples and try to lower failure rates as much as possible, but for many products that leave the manufacturer's building, there's not a 100% guarantee attached to it. So when you, the customer, buys it new, it could potentially break down after a couple of months of usage.

Retailers know that if a reconditioned product is returned, they're out even more money. So they test every product. The next time you're in the market for a home appliance, keep this in mind. There might be a model for sale that's being sold at a discount because it got scratched or dinged in transit. Or maybe it was a floor model and isn't as clean as other packaged models. Those hidden gems are possibly more reliable than the new ones they have in the back room and sell at a discount.

HOW TO INVEST IN THE "UNDERGROUND" MARKET

Trying to grow your wealth in the stock market can always be a risky proposition. So many vested parties have the ability to manipulate prices to make themselves better off, leaving you to fend for yourself. Fortunately, there is another "underground" market that could offer you a chance to make thousands without worrying about ever buying a single stock.

It's the commodities market. Rather than selling shares of various businesses and corporations, you can buy and sell actual concrete commodities like corn, soybeans, gold, and silver. The Chicago Mercantile Exchange (CME) Group is, as *The Economist* once put it, the "biggest financial exchange you've never heard of."

Though on the surface the exchange looks very similar to the New York Stock Exchange, there are subtle differences that make it unique. For example, the sellers in these markets are normally producers of whatever commodities are present in the market. Farmers normally come to sell of their harvest to speculators looking to turn a profit.

THE JOYS OF HARD CURRENCY

The paper money system that the government's created wasn't meant to make your life better. And anyone who claims that prefer it over the previous hard money back system doesn't understand the economics behind it. Allowing politicians and bureaucrats inject politics into the monetary system doomed it to failure from the very beginning. Once they realized that they could manipulate the money supply to create the false impression of economic growth, nothing could stop the people in power from endlessly tinkering at it.

Just because the government wants to print these green pieces of paper doesn't mean you have to play ball. The dollar isn't back by gold and silver anymore. But that doesn't mean you shouldn't purchase any. In fact, as Washington tries to print its way out of the economic mess they helped create, the need to store your wealth in another form only increases.

Luckily, there's a simple solution. Our friends at Hard Asset Alliance (http://www.hardassetsalliance.com/go/vjfta-2/LAI) offer customers the opportunity to buy, sell, and store physical gold and silver. This isn't like exchange-traded funds that offer you shares of commodities they may or may not have. The gold, silver, or any other precious metal you buy from Hard Asset Alliance are real. In fact, you can even request that it's shipped directly to you so you can hold onto it.

Because we have a business relationship with the Hard Assets Alliance, we may be compensated if you open and fund your account. But we wouldn't mention them unless we were fans of the platform.

HOW TO TAKE PART IN AMERICA'S ENERGY BOOM REBIRTH

When the sun sets over North Dakota, strange lights fill the skies. But they're not like the lights that come from big cities like New York, Los Angeles, and Chicago. Even though these lights can be seen from space, there's no major city in this one particular spot in North Dakota. Yet it's just as bright.

On closer inspection, you'd see that these mysterious night lights are the result of energy companies burning off natural gas. Because it's not as economically profitable as the oil they obtain from the Bakken oil fields, it makes more sense to destroy it than ship it off to be sold. That's how profitable America's most recent energy rebirth has been. These companies are literally willing to burn potential revenue.

Here are three ways you can take part in this energy opportunity:

1. **Denbury Resources Inc. (DNR: NYSE)** — Denbury is the largest oil and natural gas operator in both Mississippi and Montana. It owns the largest reserves of CO2 used for enhance oil recovery (EOR) east of the Mississippi River, and also holds significant operating acreage in the Rocky Mountain and Gulf Coast regions. The company's strategic goal starts with traditional exploration, drilling, and engineering practices. Then Denbury uses new EOR techniques to recover additional volumes of oil, particularly by injecting CO2 into its wells.

2. **Cenovus (CVE: NYSE)** — Cenovus holds nearly 800,000 net acres of high-quality bitumen leases in the Athabasca and Cold Lake areas. Cenovus also holds exclusive rights to lease an additional 600,000 net acres on the Cold Lake Air Weapons Range. Most of this oil resource has never been drilled and will doubtless support production for decades.

3. **Hess Corp. (HES: NYSE)** — Hess has focused on high-impact energy exploration prospects. That means Hess looks for what it calls the "Best Basin, Best Play, Best Prospect." It's an end-to-end, scientific-based quality screening process, always looking for... well, for the "best."

The cutoff for Hess is finding oil deposits of 200 million barrels or more.

THE FARMER'S SECRET NEST EGG

Everyday farmers across America provide the people of this country with the food necessary to live and function. It's an invaluable service that easily gets overlooked in an economy so focused on services and manufacturing. But farmers and the products they produce form the necessary backbone that's essential for any country, either developed or developing, to exist.

Having said this, you'll understand why their land is one of the safest investments you could ever make. Regardless of whether the economy is booming or busting, people need to eat. So owning farm land is one of the best ways to protect your wealth from the market swings that can easily ruin a retirement nest egg. If you have the money to spare and are looking for a reliable investment vehicle that's protected even in market downturns, you should strongly consider purchasing farmland.

THE COFFEE CAN PORTFOLIO: HOW A LITTLE PATIENCE CAN GENERATE HUGE REWARDS

It all began with Robert Kirby, then a portfolio manager at Capital Group. He first wrote about the coffee can idea in fall 1984 in *The Journal of Portfolio Management*. "The coffee can portfolio concept harkens back to the Old West, when people put their valuable possessions in a coffee can and kept it under the mattress," Kirby wrote. "The success of the program depended entirely on the wisdom and foresight used to select the objects to be placed in the coffee can to begin with."

The idea is simple enough: You find the best stocks you can and let them sit for 10 years. You incur practically no costs with such a portfolio. And it is certainly easy to manage. The biggest benefit, though, is a bit more subtle and meaningful. It works because it keeps your worst instincts from hurting you.

The five stocks Chris Mayer, international investor and editor of the *Capital and Crisis* newsletter, recommends are:

1. **Kennedy Wilson (KW:nyse)**
2. **Howard Hughes Corp. (HHC:nyse)**

3. **First Citizens BancShares (FCNCA:nasdaq)**
4. **Greenlight Re (GLRE:nasdaq)**
5. **Retail Opportunity Investments Corp. (ROIC:nasdaq)**

As an added bonus, he has one additional bonus stock you should add to your coffee can: **Beneficial Mutual Bancorp (BNCL:nasdaq)**

Chris's research takes him all around the globe, looking for the best research opportunities for people looking to safely grow their wealth. As he puts it, he'd only recommend a stock if he felt comfortable recommending it to his father. So you know you're in good hands when he makes a recommendation.

For example, one of Chris' more unique (and promising) investment recommendations is for **Mongolian Growth Group (YAK:tsx; MNGGF:pink sheets)**, a development company that stands ready to take advantage of the economic boom hitting the country.

7 A REVOLUTIONARY WAY TO PRESERVE YOUR RETIREMENT NEST EGG

Our family always has Sam's Club 3-in-1 carpet cleaner on hand.

Why? We have pets, and kids. So there's always a mess somewhere that needs our attention. The 3-in-1 carpet cleaner we use makes it simple to clean up one spot left by our dog or a heavily trafficked areas used by our kids. Having one solution saves us time, money and confusion on which bottle to use for each problem area.

And no, you haven't picked up an issue of *Country Homes* by mistake… The same 3-in-1 solution our family uses to keep our carpets clean is like the three-pronged strategy we've found to help you protect and safely grow your retirement.

Here's what I mean.

Recently, we surveyed readers asking "What are your biggest concerns right now?" No. 1 was government, No. 2 was retirement and No. 3 was higher taxes.

The subject of this report addresses all of those major concerns in spades… and then some. Specifically, our investment alternative will help you:

- Protect your savings from the tax man — but it's not a qualified retirement plan
- Gain stock market upside with absolutely ZERO downside… guaranteed.
- Add a layer of protection from retirement confiscation — the likes of which recently swept over Cyprus…

In short, if you're worried the U.S. is fast becoming a higher tax zone… if record stock market gains have you wondering "how long can the good times last?… or if you're nervous about the threat of government confiscation of your 401(k), IRA and regular old savings accounts, this report is for you.

An ideal solution we've uncovered works around both 401(k) confiscation <u>and</u> the dangers of market crashes. We detail it in full below, complete with charts to help you weigh your options and decide how to keep your money out of the government's greedy paws.

The time to prepare is now… let's start exploring the most devious threat of them all.

THREAT NO. 1: GOVERNMENT CONFISCATION OF SAVINGS

It's already happened. It'll happen again. And, no, we're not talking about Argentina… but Cyprus and Italy. Maybe Spain, and then France… before striking here. At any rate, the first domino has fallen.

In this environment, you need to find alternatives for your savings now more than ever. As we're about to reveal, confiscation — though downplayed in most mainstream press — could become the policy rule for the next decade right here at home. It could hit your bank account, your 401(k) and your IRA.

The U.S. has placed a stamp of approval on this scheme abroad (as we'll detail below). We wonder how long until they bring it to our shores… We want you to be prepared and have plenty of choices to protect your money — tax-advantaged too.

People in Cyprus face capital controls. They can't withdraw more than 300 euros per day — about $390. And they've been asked to fork over their own deposits to bail out the banks. That's why all eyes should be on Cyprus right now.

What the politicians and bankers are offering as "solutions" will, out of necessity, make you seek shelter for your hard-earned dough outside of the regular banking channels. Besides, the central bank gives us no hope of real interest on deposits for the next decade. But first, welcome to confiscation's test ground: Cyprus.

WELCOME TO GROUND ZERO OF A CONFISCATION CRISIS – WHERE'S NEXT?

Original estimates to bail out Cyprus (and its banks) were 17.5 billion euros. But that proved too low. Try 23 billion euros, or more than the entire GDP of Cyprus. So that's why they capped the banking freedoms of its citizenry and went for their cash! Anyone with deposits of more than 100,000 euros will lose some of their savings. As we're writing, this it looks like the "confiscation" cut is huge. Imagine if you had 500,000 euros, and you — like the Bank of Cyprus' savers — lost 47.5% of it. That's 237,500 euros gone! Or over $317,325 vanished forever. And the unlucky who banked at Laiki Bank lost everything over 100,000 euros.

Yet the Cypriot government is still scrambling for what to seize or sell next. They're onto discussing raiding the nation's gold reserves... Meanwhile, plenty of Cypriots can't even touch their own money...

So now, 90% of uninsured depositors' money is currently frozen, with a vague promise that they'll regain access. It can't be touched until the Cyprus Central Bank gets notice from the real committee controlling this deal (based in London — more below). This money is fair game for whole or partial confiscation — ahem — "conversion" as they call it — because savers might get a forced to hold shares in the Bank of Cyprus. Right now, Cypriots hardly know where they stand. And it's not their government that's calling the shots.

HOW THE FDIC AND THE BANK OF ENGLAND SOLD OUT CYPRUS... AND LEFT THE DOOR OPEN TO CONFISCATE

The big guns — the FDIC and the Bank of England — have already written the rules for Cyprus' playbook. And they snuck it quietly into a little "joint paper" where they thought no one would notice it.

Page 1 opens by saying:

The Federal Deposit Insurance Corporation (FDIC) and the Bank of England — together with the Board of Governors of the Federal Reserve System, the Federal Reserve Bank of New York and the Financial Services Authority — have been working to develop resolution strategies for the failure of globally active, systemically important, financial institutions (SIFIs or G-SIFIs) with significant operations on both sides of the Atlantic.

The goal is to produce resolution strategies that could be implemented for the failure of one or more of the largest financial institutions with extensive activities in our respective jurisdictions. These resolution strategies should maintain systemically important operations and contain threats to financial stability. They should also assign losses to shareholders and unsecured creditors in the group, thereby avoiding the need for a bailout by taxpayers.

This joint paper goes on to prove that authority to implement such solutions is already in place. Dodd-Frank in the U.S. In the U.K., the base of powers comes from the U.K. Banking Act of 2009. "Such a strategy," it emphasizes "would involve the bail-in (write-down or conversion) of creditors at the top of the group in order to restore the whole group to solvency."

Further, pages 4–5, detail how this "bail in" process works to screw over deposit holders first and foremost.

> The introduction of a statutory bail-in resolution tool (the power to write down or convert into equity the liabilities of a failing firm) under the RRD [European Union Recovery and Resolution Directive] is critical to implementing a whole group resolution of U.K. firms in a way that reduces the risks to financial stability. A bail-in tool would enable the U.K. authorities to recapitalize an institution by *allocating losses to its shareholders and unsecured creditors,* thereby avoiding the need to split or transfer operating entities. The provisions in the RRD that enable the resolution authority to impose a temporary stay on the exercise of termination rights by counterparties in the event of a firm's entry into resolution (in other words, preventing counterparties from terminating their contractual arrangements with a firm solely as a result of the firm's entry into resolution) will be needed to ensure the bail-in is executed in an orderly manner.

Further, it assured it'd be easy to "expand the scope of the Banking Act to include [nondeposit-taking firms]" — think investment banks and clearing houses…Parliament agreed. House of Commons gave the updated Financial Services Bill the final OK on Dec. 10, 2012. Royal Assent came on the 19th.

On the U.S. front, The FDIC leads the charge:

> To capitalize the new operations — one or more new private entities — the FDIC expects that it will have to look to subordinated debt or

even senior unsecured debt claims as the immediate source of capital. The original debt holders can thus expect that their claims will be written down to reflect any losses in the receivership of the parent that the shareholders cannot cover and that, like those of the shareholders, these claims will be left in the receivership.

At this point, the remaining claims of the debt holders will be converted, in part, into equity claims that will serve to capitalize the new operations. The debt holders may also receive convertible subordinated debt in the new operations. This debt would provide a cushion against further losses in the firm, as it can be converted into equity if needed. Any remaining claims of the debt holders could be transferred to the new operations in the form of new unsecured debt.

In short, if even senior credit holders can be caught in the crossfire, you can bet that the lowly deposit holder has no position of standing. As we've happen in Cyprus.

It's just come out as we're wrapping up our report that 47.5% of the uninsured deposits (those over 100,000 euros) will undergo forced conversion — that's 10% higher than decided earlier in 2013. These deposit holders will now get Class A shares in the new bank their old bank is being folded into (aka the bail-in). The only nice part of the deal? Class A shares have voting rights. And dividends — if or when the new bank makes money after restructuring…

For us in the U.S., the outlined solution promises that anything over the $250,000 mark in the U.S. is fair game for confiscation.

Finally, the double-talking bankers dare to say on Page 11 (under the "Maintaining Financial Stability" header):

Similarly, because the group remains solvent, retail or corporate depositors **should not have an incentive to "run" from the firm** under resolution insofar as their banking arrangements, transacted at the operating company level, remain unaffected. **In order to achieve this, the authorities recognize the need for effective communication to depositors, making it clear that their deposits will be protected."** [emphasis added].

In short, convince everyone their deposits are safe… even if they are subject to confiscation.

Recently, the looniezone announced a confiscation-ready plan of its own. Buried on Page144 of its 2013 Canadian Economic Action Plan (aka the budget), you can find this comment: "requires strong prudential oversight and a robust set of options for resolving these institutions without the use of taxpayer funds, in the unlikely event that one becomes nonviable."

So that means — you got it — using depositor funds instead of taxpayer funds. No more 2008-like strategies this time… although none of the institutions is any less "too big to fail" than before the crisis.

Second, on the next page, the Canuck government "proposes to implement a bail-in regime for systematically important banks.…The bank can be recapitalized and returned to viability through a very rapid conversion of certain bank liabilities into regulatory capital. This will reduce risk for taxpayers," the plan assures. As if a taxpayer is not likely to be a depositor as well!

So you shouldn't be surprised that the force behind the Cyprus bank bail-in is none other than the Prudential Regulation Authority — a quasi-government arm of the Bank of England that has its fingerprints all over the Cyprus deal.

FIRST CYPRUS, NEXT UP ITALY…

Now they're getting wise to STEALING depositors' money, deposit insurance be damned. Italy is ready to support the next deposit heist…

The head chief of Italy's largest bank, UniCredit, very publicly ventured that "It is acceptable to confiscate savings to save banks." We hope that's an error in translation. Did he happily say the dreaded word: "confiscate"?

Uninsured bank deposits, says Federico Ghizzoni, are fair game to rescue ailing banks — under the assumption that global policymakers make such "measures" uniform. Meaning it's OK if we're ALL going to do it.

Bloomberg continues the story:

Ghizzoni urged that the Cyprus model be adopted as a "common solution in Europe," and that the EU "should pass laws identical and shared in different member states" — and that similar rules should be imposed on the global banking system. While seizing private deposits is appropriate, Ghizzoni claimed, "What we cannot accept is differentiation country by country."

He urges that these measures extend beyond the EU, to "the Basel Committee, where all countries are represented. Otherwise we would open the market for arbitrage."

True. Can't have that. Bad banking policy for all — or else folks will go where their money is safest. And true enough, we've just seen that Brazil, in the wake of eight bank failures of its own, is adding its own endorsement for the new "bail in" plan.

Here at home, even a Fed governor admits the truth. Jeremy Stein made a speech "Regulating Large Financial Institutions" in which he says, if and when a big bank fails, depositors will hold the bag. To quote Mr. Stein: "I have little doubt that private investors will, in fact, bear the losses — even if it leads to an outcome that is messier and more costly to society than we would ideally like."

What's to blame, according to Stein? Thank Dodd-Frank. "Dodd-Frank is very clear in saying that the Federal Reserve and other regulators *cannot use their emergency authorities to bail out a failing institution*. As a member of the board," he says, "I am committed to following both the letter and the spirit of the law."

Well, America, consider yourself warned.

Chances are, you might well be a "small depositor" — but you might also one day end up in the boat of exceeding your depositor's insurance.

And in fact, if we do a little back-of-the-envelope math, you'll see that there's a mere $25 billion in the FDIC piggy bank set aside for ensuring your deposits.

Compare that to $9,283 billion — that's $9.3 trillion — in deposits at the various U.S. banks.

Better hope there's only one failure…

UNDER ATTACK: BANK DEPOSITS AND NOW 401(K)S AND IRAS

Savings accounts in Cyprus have already been pillaged. Now here in the good ole US of A, our 401(k)s and IRAs are increasingly under attack by Washington. Whatever these accounts are doing for you now, it's likely that 20, 30 or 50 years from now — just when you need them most — the rules will change.

Consider the president's recent budget proposal: to cap lifetime contributions to retirement accounts. Some dismiss it, saying, "it's only affecting people who have over $3 million stashed in a retirement account" — like presidential nominee Mitt Romney, with his $100 million-plus IRA. Sure, we have no love lost on him... but keep in mind this is the first step to what could become a continual process of re-evaluating the structure of so-called tax-advantaged retirement accounts.

Here's the creepy call to arms from the White House in an April 5 statement: "Under current rules, some wealthy individuals" can accumulate "substantially more than is needed to fund reasonable levels of retirement savings." That $3 million, by the by, gives an annuity of $205,000.

Sure gives us here at *Apogee* the willies.

Who is my government to define the dollar amount I need to enjoy my retirement? The typical household circa 2010 has about $120,000 in a 401(k) or IRA. Does that mean I should be handicapped in what I can save to "enjoy" the same standard of living as they might?

This kind of thing is our beat here at *Apogee*, and we'll be looking out for the future attacks levied on these accounts. But in the meantime, we've got one diversifying strategy you can employ that doesn't involve a bank account, and IRA or a 401(k).

One multifaceted product offers you a plethora of protections. But I'll warn you, it's not a product for everyone. Luckily, after you read this report, we're giving you a second source for you to bounce questions off of.

But before we get to that, let's cover the second major threat to your standard of living:

THREAT NO. 2: RISING STOCK MARKET VOLATILITY

Chances are you're sick of stomach-lurching headlines like "Stocks Sink on Fed Worries After Record Highs; Dow Down Triple Digits."

These headlines work so well because we all worry that record highs are too good to be true... And that's all thanks to the Fed. You'll see other headlines like "VIX Pops as Markets Go Wobbly Over Fed Minutes."

Then you read something like: "The Chicago Board Options Exchange Volatility Index — the So-called 'Fear Index' Popped...as U.S. Markets Saw a Sharp Sell-off."

Here's the story the VIX has told since 2008.

When the VIX starts to trend toward 20, that's when you should start to worry... however, the solution we'll get to below keeps you from having to watch the VIX in its nail-biting moments or asking yourself to time the market perfectly.

John Bogle, who created the second-largest mutual fund company in the world, famously said, "I never met anyone who can successfully time the market. I never met anyone who knows anyone who can successfully time the market."

So as a small investor, your best bet is not to spend all your energy (and capital) trying to time the market. The three-in-one solution we'll share addresses this problem two ways: 1) offering indexed strategies with a floor under you — guaranteeing a 1% return, say; 2) Giving you the option of looking back on the past years' market performance… and then getting your return.

THREAT NO. 3: RISING TAX ENVIRONMENT

Who's not afraid of mounting taxes?

On June 29, 2012, The Supreme Court officially condoned Obamacare as a tax on America. The vote was close, admittedly at 5–4, but yes, they declared Congress has the authority to levy this tax. "The financial penalty," wrote Chief Justice Roberts, for failing to carry insurance, possesses "the essential feature of any tax." — it produces government revenue.

However, there's more than the one tax…

Do you make more than $200,000? Pay a 3.8% surtax on your investment income. What's considered "investment income?" Dividends that you love the collect. Rents that diversify your income stream. Annuities. Capital gains. Sell a house?

You're paying more for Medicare — 0.9% more if you make more than $200,000.

Want to take money out of your HSA? That'll be double the old penalty of 10%.

Lucky enough to have a "Cadillac health plan" still? In 2018 and beyond, you'll start paying a 40% tax.

FactCheck.org added these taxes altogether and — based on your income —calculated how much you can expect to pay as Obamacare comes into full force.

Basically, you're looking at tax penalties in this ballpark (depending on your income):

- Make $50,000? You'll pay an extra $1,000
- Make $150,000? Cut that by an additional $3,500
- Make $200,000? Part with $4,700 more.

That's this year's affront on the taxpayer. Next, we can expect higher income taxes on the way...

Right now, we've got the fourth highest income tax rate in the world (kicking in when you earn over $44,000) at 44%. Spain, for example, sweeps over half its citizens' income into its coffers every year.

Why so high? Well, think about it. Spain suffers from three things: recession, chronic ballooning deficit, and increasing investor doubt about its sovereign debt.

Sound familiar? Yes, we've got those problems too. Consider our debt-to-GDP that's topped 100% (101.6% as of the end of year 2012 reckoning). Spain's was around 85%.

Moody's, for example, downgraded the sovereign credit rating of our friends across the pond in the U.K. — knocking them down from the coveted "safe" AAA. Moody's has us on watch, but Standard & Poor's already stripped our AAA status. The third big ratings agency — Fitch — warned Congress that it has to get budget cuts in order, or else... Fitch already followed Moody's lead and stripped the U.K. of its AAA as well. Are we next?

However, we expect this tax hike to happen first: Dividend income being taxed as ordinary income. As you get older, you'll be trusting dividends to offer you some extra quality of living...

As the fiscal cliff of 2012 drew nigh, the president called for nearly tripling the dividend tax for any family bringing in over $250,000 per year — a 43.4% rate. The "fiscal cliff compromise" settled on a 20% rate — versus the old 15% — if you made more than $400,000 a year (or $450,000 for the married folk). Seems like it's only a matter of time for the sheltered dividends to become ordinary income...

And these aren't the only taxes creeping up on us... cigarette taxes... the IRA heist we detailed above... increased scrutiny of any of us who live part time abroad and how we make our living. It's all getting tighter, but we give you a way to slip the government noose from your savings below...

THE GREAT 3-IN-1 SOLUTION: BEAT THREE RETIREMENT KILLERS AT ONCE

We've sniffed out a new strategy that isn't even on Washington's radar (it's a small pool of cash compared with savings accounts and qualified retirement plans). And it's the ultimate tool if you want to get your money off the "sidelines" — but are worried about the next crash.

So if I told you:

1. Don't fear higher taxes.
2. Forget bracing for a stock market crash.
3. Ignore government retirement confiscation of your 401(k).

You'd be pretty happy, right?

Well, that's precisely what today's breed of indexed universal life insurance policies (IULs) allow you to do. About 100 companies now offer these plans, and there are plenty of differences between them. We'll share with you some of our favorites. First, at the risk of your eyes glazing over, let's quickly cover two basic facets of "cash value" life insurance policies.

When you pay your annual life insurance premium, part of that payment goes to pay the cost of insuring your life (i.e., the insurance company putting money aside to pay your beneficiary the death benefit).

The remainder of your premium payment gets credited to your policy — called the cash value. Think of it as insurance for the worst-case scenario with a reservoir of savings.

It's what happens to this cash value that makes the indexed universal life policies so interesting.

Here are the benefits an indexed universal life policy (IUL) provides.

1. Upside stock market potential — PLUS — a guaranteed floor that protects your money — even if the stock market goes nowhere or collapses.

2. Legally borrow funds from your account TAX-FREE.

3. Your cash value is invested outside of a qualified retirement account, so you don't get stuck paying early withdrawal fees or penalties if you need the money before you reach 62½. Plus, since Washington is laser-focused on the $10

trillion sitting in qualified retirement accounts — IRAs and 401(k)s — the cash value in a life insurance policy if off D.C.'s radar.

Let's cover the core reason IULs are growing faster than any other life insurance product in the U.S.

NO.1: UPSIDE STOCK MARKET POTENTIAL PLUS A GUARANTEED FLOOR PROTECTING YOUR SAVINGS

We love it when the market goes up. Last year, the S&P 500 shot up over 13%. Add in dividends and you saw a 16% performance. Great year!

But what about when the market falls, or crashes — like it did in the dot-com crash?

Add up the portfolio catastrophe: 2000 (-9.11%)

2001 (-11.89%)
2002 (-22.10%)
_____
= -43% total damage.

By 2005, you might have been back in the black… just in time for the next bubble. In 2008, we saw a 38.5% drop in a single year! Those are beatings no one wants to take.

So here's where your indexed universal life insurance plan comes into play. Depending on the plan you choose, you can protect your cash value (savings) from market drops, *guaranteed*.

In the insurance biz, this safety net is called the **floor**. Your returns for any given year will never be lower than the floor in your policy. Some have a floor of 0%, others 1% and even 2%.

That means if you have $100,000 in cash value in your account, a floor of 1% and the markets drop 10% in a given year… your cash value will grow by $1,000. This provision is especially important in years where the markets can cut investments by 20%, 30% and even 40%.

Of course, with guaranteed downside, you have to give something up. And that's upside, or in the insurance world, a **ceiling**. The ceiling varies depending on the carrier and commonly ranges from 10–13%. So if the markets go up 25% in a given policy year, the most your cash value can grow is the amount of your ceiling, or 10–13%. Each carrier has different strategies for both floors and ceilings.

And here's something a lot of people don't know. You can actually put more money into your life insurance policy than your annual premium payment. This strategy is called **overfunding**. And while there are limits to how much you can put into your policy, it can be an attractive investment alternative in low interest rate environments like we face today.

Whatever you decide to do, it's important you discuss your particular needs with a trusted licensed insurance professional.

As you look over the table above… note that the cash value your IUL plan accumulates based on an index: The S&P 500 is the most prolific, but the more exciting plans offer you choices.

Now that you see how the IUL can protect your savings — while giving you upside potential — let's discuss how you can get access to these funds without having to pay the IRS… legally.

NO.2: TAX-FREE FEATURES AND PRE-RETIREMENT ACCESS – WITHOUT PAYING EARLY WITHDRAWAL FEES

As with any cash-value life insurance policy, indexed universal life offers features you can't get from ordinary investments… tax-advantaged investment gains.

Here's what that means.

First, as your cash value grows inside your policy, the gains are not taxed. So you don't have to worry if your account grows by 7% next year… Uncle Sam does not get his pound of flesh from your life insurance policy. But here's what's even better…

If you ever need to pull money out of your policy, you won't pay taxes on the gains either! This is allowed through a loan provision allowed within life insurance policies. Here's an example…

Imagine your daughter has met the love of her life and has decided to tie the knot. Weddings, as you know, can be expensive. And if you're on the hook for throwing a party for 120 people, you might need access to some reserve cash. What do you do?

If you're under 59½, you can't gain access to your retirement accounts without paying a 10–20% penalty. Ouch.

However, if you have a cash-value life insurance policy, you can **take out a withdrawal or a loan from your policy** and spend it how you like. No penalties. No taxes. You get a check from your insurance company free from federal, state, local and alternative minimum taxes.

It's spelled out in the Internal Revenue Code Section 7702 and 7702A. So ultimately, IULs provide you with flexible access to your money for retirement. While you will need to pay interest on the loan each year (% varies by carrier and policy type), it's much less than IRA early withdrawal fees. Loan provisions help you access your money without having to pay taxes on the profits… and it's all legal.

NO. 3: CONFISCATION-PROOFING FROM CONGRESS

Right now the U.S. — thanks to its growing debt burden — has huge promises to keep, especially to China and Japan. Nationalizing retirement accounts is a one way of borrowing even more from us the U.S.' largest debtor, with the upshot that it won't devalue our currency.

Early on, the fear about a tax-favored account like an IRA or a 401(k) was that when the pool of our savings grew large enough, Congress would not be able to keep their paws off.

This past year, we're starting to find out those fears are justified.

We've already seen the president propose a cap to tax-deferred retirement contributions. Again, he says the cap is enough to give a 62 year old the amount needed to buy an annuity that generates $205,000 a year. Screw anyone who can put away more than that…

How many savers would be impacted? Well, the Employee Benefit Research Institute says 0.06% of IRA holders have more than $3 million. Similarly, 1 in 25,000 have a 401(k) account in excess of $3 million.

That said, these things always start small… and get bigger. That $10 trillion (and growing) in U.S. IRAs and 401(k)s is way too tempting…

We've been alerting readers to the warning signs on confiscation since our September 2012 Issue. The first warning sign — "Eliminating the Tax-Advantage"— sounded. Two red-alert indicators in the realm of state and local pensions, as well as private, will let us know when the jig is up.

Meanwhile, life insurance policies aren't in Congress' cross-hairs. After all, the whole point of giving life insurance tax favorable treatment is the idea that families should be encouraged to protect themselves financially from the unexpected loss of the family breadwinner (and keeping people off of so-called entitlement programs).

Interestingly enough, the WSJ reports that the top 10% of the nation's highest-income earners own 55% of the investment gains built up in life insurances policies, which means that they have plenty of faith in the taxfreeness of this avenue. We expect they'll help keep it that way…

Speaking of investment gains, let's explore the innovative new feature that has really put IULs popularity on a rocket ship trajectory…

BONUS: WELCOME TO THE TRUE POWER OF DIVERSITY & HINDSIGHT

Some readers would like to worry less about their investments as they get older… while others would like to hone strategy once retired and day trade with abandon. But if you're in the former camp, here's why we think you'll especially like the indexed universal life policy.

Which of the following stock indexes do you think had the most No. 1 finishes when comparing annual returns since 1992? The Hang Seng, Euro Stoxx or the good ol' American S&P 500?

Try the Hang Seng. Yup, it beat the Euro Stoxx and S&P whopping 72% of the time. And the S&P? Finished in first place only 7% of the time.

Pretty unexpected, eh?

So wouldn't it be great to not have to "guess" which market is going to outperform which year?

That's now a reality with the "look back" feature. Here's how it works.

INVESTING HINDSIGHT SECURES YOUR RETIREMENT FUTURE: THE LOOK-BACK FEATURE

One of the most interesting policies — from ING — allows your cash value to be "indexed" against three different stock indexes. That simply means the returns in this policy will mimic how those indexes perform… but with a twist.

Rather than sticking your hopes to the performance of the ol' S&P 500, ING's plan offers global diversity. ING adds the Hang Seng and the Euro Stoxx 50.

Now here's where the "look back" comes into play. When the insurance company tallies up your return at the end of the year, it "looks back" over the entire year's performance of the three indexes. Rather than give you the sum of the performances… it stacks the deck in your favor.

Just like striking the low score from an Olympian's point total, this feature drops the performance of the weakest performing index altogether. You'll get 75% of the best performing index, plus 25% of the next best performing index.

For example, say the Hang Seng beats the Euro Stoxx 50. And that the S&P actually got a negative return. That negative return won't count against you. Instead, you'd get three-quarters of your return calculated from the Hang Seng and one-quarter from Euro Stoxx.

This is a great feature… giving you a real advantage when it comes to securing your wealth. But not all plans offer the look back. Some seek simply to diversify.

Finally, there's one other consideration when calculating your returns. It's called the participation rate. The participation rate determines how much of the gain in the index will be credited to your policy's cash value. The higher the participation rate, the better for you, the policyholder.

For example, the insurance company may set the participation rate at 80%, which means your cash value would be credited with 80% of the gain experienced by the index.

Consider this example. Say you chose a policy with a 75% participation rate. If the underlying index (i.e., the S&P 500) increased by 10%, you would receive 75% of that 10% gain — a 7.5% rate of return on your money that year.

But you might be wondering what's the deal on the participation rate versus the cap rate? Well, they're two sides of the same coin. Different carriers use one or the other (but not both). Typically, the capped policy offers less upside over time… but it's also a less expensive policy. You'll likely pay more for a plan that uses a participation rate, but your upside potential will be higher over the long run.

THINGS TO KEEP IN MIND AS YOU CONSIDER INDEXED UNIVERSAL LIFE

One thing to keep in mind on the policy loan front: the potential for policy lapse. Ideally, you pay premiums for a certain amount of time and then start using tax-free contract loans that are greater than the amount you paid in premium. Ultimately, the accumulated loans are paid off at death by your tax-free death benefit.

The catch is that accumulated loans could cause the contract to lapse. Should that happen, you would be taxed on the sum of cash you've taken out minus the premiums you originally paid in. So that might be a substantial lump sum! However, as you're choosing your policy, ask and be sure it has an "overloan protection rider" — most carriers will offer this — which will make sure policy lapse never happens to you.

Also, don't forget, this isn't an index product; it's not a retirement account. It's a life insurance policy. Chances are you already have a policy, but we'd be remiss not to mention this factor: the cost of insurance.

When you buy a policy, the company will levy a charge for the insurance protection upon death and to cover administrative expenses. Call it the actual costs of your insurance. It'll be deducted from your policy's account value per month.

Your insurance pro will give you a table spelling out these charges. However, what you pay now may not be the same as what you'll pay down the road. Most companies reserve the right to change these charges over the duration of your policy. The rule of thumb you can count on is that the older you are, the more you'll pay.

Finally, let's just talk for a minute about surrender charges. The surrender charge is the fee you pay should you cancel your life insurance policy. Obviously, the same insurer wants to keep your business. Hence, the charge. And if you withdraw or take out a loan more than the penalty-free amount from the cash balance on your policy, you'll get hit with a surrender charge. Fortunately, there is a limit on the time the insurance company has to assess these fees.

And here's one difference between indexed universal life policies and others: The surrender period is longer. Typical insurance plans range from three–eight years. When you take out an indexed universal life policy, you're going to have to stay in it a little longer say 10–15 years to avoid surrender charges. Note that during the surrender period you can't take a withdrawal at all. In the rare cases when you can, it's limited to one. However, once you're out of the surrender period, you'll have no charges on withdrawals.

Naturally, each policy will have different specifics, and it's in your best interest to understand everything the insurer presents.

While indexed universal life insurance isn't something to make your sole "retirement" strategy, it can help you diversify your retirement savings risk.

8 HOW TO BUILD A HEALTHIER YOU

Trusting the government to take care of you when you need it most is just setting yourself up to be disappointed. The government's track record on helping those in need is dismal. Making sure you live a happy healthy life means that you need to put yourself in charge of your own personal well-being.

But it doesn't mean you shouldn't get some help. Check out these simple solutions and ideas that will give you more control over how you live your life.

THE NATURAL NO STIMULANT ENERGY BOOST

Every day, millions of Americans pumps gallons upon gallons of coffee and other stimulants into their bodies to help get them through the day. People's addiction to caffeine has fueled an entire industry. But studies are slowly coming out detailing the negative effects of too much caffeine in the body.

In response, avid coffee drinkers have tried to cut back or at least have made the switch over to decaffeinated. In the end, however, they lose the energy boost.

Fortunately, there are alternatives to chemical stimulants to get you through the day. Societies throughout history have discovered ingenious ways to exploit the body's natural design. For example, traditional Chinese medicine has shown that massaging certain pressure points in your body increases blood circulation in the body. This, in turn, helps you generate more energy, giving you that added kick when you need it most.

One of the best parts of your body to massage when you're feeling low on energy is your ears. They're especially sensitive because they're packed with pressure points. Rubbing your entire ear with your palms for at least one minute will give you a shot of energy comparable to cup of coffee!

THE BEST WORKOUT YOU CAN DO WITHOUT WEIGHTS

Turn on the TV today and before long, you're bound to come across an infomercial advertising the latest exercise craze, whether it's promoting the benefits of hip-hop aerobics or a state-of-the-art home gym that will save you thousands of dollars.

But before you break out your credit card, here's a quick workout routine that you can do in your own home without the use of any fancy equipment:

1. First, run in place to raise your heart rate and warm your body up. Mix things up by throwing in some jumping jacks.

2. **Squats (1 minute)** — Starting with your feet shoulder distance apart and your hands behind your head, slowly lower down into a squat position. Make sure your knees don't extend beyond your toes, and distribute your weight evenly.

3. **Pushups (1 minute)** — Depending on your fitness level, you might have to begin this workout with angled standing pushups off a counter or table. As your progress, you can move on to knee pushups and, finally, standard pushups.

4. **Plank (1 minute)** — At first, this might seem like an easy position. But holding it for 60 seconds will soon make you realize how necessary having a strong core is. In a position similar to standard pushup, lower down onto your forearms. Your body weight should be evenly distributed between your forearms and your toes, and your legs and back should form a straight line.

5. **Stairs** — Find a set of stairs in your house or apartment building and set a goal in your head. Whether it's two flights

or 10, push yourself, but also know your limits. Don't wear yourself out, because when you're done, you have to do everything all over again.

The key to this workout is remaining consistent with your timing and not wearing yourself out in the first round. In the beginning, you might find yourself taking many breaks, but as you progress, you'll notice yourself getting stronger as your body gets used to the routine.

STRESSFREE LIVING

In today's world of endless bills and obligations, it's easy to become overwhelmed. If you're like most Americans, you've dealt with the problems of stress at some point in your life. Turning to traditional drugs or medicine, or nontraditional solutions like alcohol, will provide only temporary relief. They mask the effects of stress without dealing with the problem itself.

Prolonged reliance on these methods to reducing stress might damage the nervous system and impair your ability to deal with stress in the long run.

Thankfully, there are natural solutions to this problem, ones that won't cause you to develop bad habits that might negatively affect your life in the future.

There is a breathing technique called diaphragmatic breathing (DB) that helps oxygenate the organs in your body, which provokes a more rapid release of toxins, helping you to relax. Instead of breathing short, fairly rapid breaths with just your chest, DB moves your diaphragm as well as your stomach.

Starting from either a sitting or lying position, place one hand on your stomach and the other on your chest. Take a slow, deep breath and make sure that as your chest fills, your stomach retracts toward your spine. Once your lungs are filled, pause for a moment before exhaling as slowly as you inhaled. Once you feel your lungs completely empty, pause for a moment before beginning your next breath.

The technique sounds simple on paper, but you might soon find it difficult once you try it yourself. Listen to your body and don't push yourself if you feel uncomfortable. Like most exercises, your body will adjust the more you practice. Hopefully, you'll reach a point where the length of each breath is the same.

Whenever you feel the pangs of stress creeping in your daily life, take a five-minute break and practice this breathing technique. You can do it in your office chair, waiting for a doctor's appointment, or even while stuck in traffic.

MAKE SURE YOUR MEDICINE CABINET IS STOCKED

It's the middle of the night. Your stomach wakes you suddenly, and you stumble to your bathroom looking for anything that could give you relief. The question is whether you have the right medicine among the countless bottles in your medicine cabinet.

With all the different options available to you at your local drugstore, it's easy to get lost in the sea of over-the-counter medicines. Many drugs are meant to take care of specific ailments. But then there are some that cover a handful and can be useful when symptoms pile up. Taking a minimalist approach and stockpiling the most essential medicines will help you get through the clutter and ensure you have the right medicine should you find yourself in pain in the middle of the night.

Here's a list of eight medicines/medical supplies you should have in your cabinet:

1. Aspirin
2. Acetaminophen
3. Ibuprofen
4. Muscle rub ointments (e.g., Icy Hot, Tiger Balm, etc.)
5. Triple antibiotic ointment (e.g., Neosporin)
6. Hydrogen peroxide
7. Stool softener (e.g., laxative)
8. Pepto-Bismol

These shouldn't be the only things in your cabinet. But similar to how any tool chest should have a hammer, screwdriver, and a set of pliers, it's a start. Having these eight things handy will solve many common problems. Once they're covered, you can start fine-tuning your cabinet based on specific personal medical conditions and ailments.

THE BEST WAY TO PREVENT A HEART ATTACK

One of the most common (and frightening) statistics when it comes to heart attacks is that one-third of all first-time heart attack victims don't survive.

With that in mind, there are things you can do today to increase your chances of surviving a heart attack. Since most heart attacks happen within three hours of waking up, it's essential to make sure you have the right things in your home. World-renowned heart surgeon Dr. Mehmet Oz recommends doing the following:

1. Using a small compact mirror, check to see if you have three of these four hidden signs. They could indicate you're at a higher risk of a heart attack: a crease in one of your earlobes, receding hairline at the temples, a bald patch at the top of your head, yellow fatty deposits around the eyes.

2. Decrease your chances of a heart attack by keeping vitamin D handy. It can help regulate blood pressure, inflammation and blood sugar. The recommended daily dosage is 1,000 IUs every morning.

3. If you think you might be having a heart attack, take a 325-mg tablet of adult aspirin. To get the drug into your bloodstream faster, chew it, instead of swallowing.

4. Keeping a cellphone or installing a telephone in your bath-room could save your life. If you realize you're having a heart attack, every second counts.

YOUR BODY IS A TEMPLE, HERE'S HOW TO MAINTAIN IT

Rising blood pressure is another common problem among Americans. Many people turn to prescription medicine to help get it under control. Thankfully, there are other natural methods that don't require the use of drugs. It's important that you discuss all available options with your doctor before deciding on the best course of action. With that in mind, here are some natural solutions to hypertension.

Starting and maintaining a daily exercise routine could help lower blood pressure significantly. It doesn't have to be something extremely strenuous. In fact, finding something that you enjoy could increase the chance that you stick to your routine. It could be something as simple as walking or running for 30 minutes three or four times a week.

Going hand in hand with a daily exercise routine, losing weight has shown to have a positive effect on blood pressure. The extra pounds you carry with you every day add stress to your heart, causing your body to work harder. Lightening the cardiovascular load could be the best and most effective way to get your hypertension under control.

You might be aware that salt and sodium raise blood pressure. But did you know that potassium helps counteract those ill effects? Unfortunately, most Americans don't get enough potassium in their daily diets. Adding some ordinary but high in potassium items to your daily diet can help get your hypertension under control. A few examples of these foods include bananas, baked potatoes with the skin, orange juice, and nonfat yogurt.

If you're a smoker, now might be a good time to think about quitting. Besides all the other negative effects associated with smoking, tobacco and nicotine can cause temporary spikes in your blood pressure.

DON'T LET THAT COLD GET YOU DOWN

The common cold. A disease that has plagued humanity throughout most of its existence. One that mutates and transforms constantly, making it practically impossible to find a cure. But just because there isn't a cure doesn't mean you have to suffer once you feel it coming on. There are plenty of natural remedies you can use to help alleviate any pain and suffering.

Make sure you blow your nose the right way. To avoid building up pressure in your ears, don't blow both nostrils at the same time. Instead, close off one while gently blowing through the other. And make sure you wash your hands afterward to prevent spreading any germs.

If it's possible, call in sick. Today, many people try to power through sickness and do anything to avoid missing work. But there are many reasons why you should stay in bed when you're in the middle of a cold. First of all, your employer might not want you in the office. Having one sick employee is one thing. But having that person spread the cold to other staff members is far worse. Additionally, rest is one of the most effective ways to get over any sickness.

Since you'll be home all day, make sure you gargle often. You heard that right. Gargling is an effective way of relieving a sore throat and brings temporary relief to any nagging symptoms. Gargling a tea that contains tannin will help relieve a tickle in your throat. If that's not available, use a mixture of honey and apple cider vinegar. Just make sure anything you gargle is either cool or room temperature. The last thing you want to do is trade your sore throat for a scalded one.

Utilize the benefits of a steam room. If you don't have access at your local gym, you can always turn your bathroom into one. Turn on the hot water, start the shower, close the door, and let the water run for five–10 minutes. Once enough steam is built up, take a seat and allow it to loosen your sinuses. For an added benefit, sit in the shower itself (be care and don't get burned by the hot water) to intensify the level of steam.

EMERGENCY MIGRAINE SOLUTIONS

If you've ever experienced a migraine, you know it's something that should be avoided at all costs. Prevention is always preferable, and maintaining a healthy lifestyle with regular exercise can contribute to that. Controlling the amount of stress in your life can also lower your chances of experiencing a migraine.

Taking supplements is another method used to prevent migraines. Each person is different, so you have to try different combinations to see which works best for you. Here are four common supplements that are available: butterbur root (or Petasites), vitamin B2, coenzyme Q10, and magnesium.

If prevention isn't possible and you find yourself stuck in the middle of a full-blown migraine, there are medicines that could help alleviate the worst symptoms. Over-the-counter nonsteroidal anti-inflammatory medicines like naproxen and ibuprofen inhibit blood vessel inflammation. And drugs like Excedrin combine acetaminophen and caffeine to narrow blood vessels and increase the effectiveness of pain medication.

HOW TO KEEP YOUR BRAIN SHARP

Doing a Sudoku puzzle every day isn't the only way to keep your brain healthy. In fact, like many things concerning your body, what you put into it greatly affects what you get out of it. Your brain is a muscle. And making sure you provide it with the right foods and nutrients will ensure that it stays sharp and healthy as you get older.

But it's not as if you can simply eat more protein to strengthen your brain. It requires specific foods that will promote healthy brain function. Here's a list of five food options recommended by Dr. Joseph Mercola and Rachael Droege that will keep your mind sharp:

1. **Krill oil** — About 60% of your brain is made up of fat. Bet you didn't know that. Most of this fat is either an omega-3 fatty acid called DHA or an arachidonic acid (AA). While the latter is best obtained from uncooked dairy products, you can get the former from seafood sources. Krill oil is a better alternative than fish because of the high mercury content found in most seafood.

2. **Organic, raw vegetables** — If you can't find organic vegetables, any vegetables will do. A good rule of thumb is to eat at least one pound of vegetables for every 50 pounds of body weight. Some good healthy options include: spinach, green beans, cauliflower, and asparagus.

3. **Avoid sugar** — This might be tough to do, since so many foods in your daily life contain some form of sugar. Things as harmless as peanut butter and tomato sauce may actually contain some level of sugar in their ingredients. But it's important to eliminate (or, if that's not possible, greatly reduce) it from your daily diet. Take small steps like cutting out soda and candy. And make sure you don't replace it with things like fruit juice. This "healthy" drink alternative is actually loaded with sugar.

4. **Blueberries** — If you can't get rid of sugar completely, know that there's always a healthy and organic alternative with blueberries. They're also one of the most powerful antioxidants you can consume. Some studies have even shown that they can reverse the effects of aging that occurs in the brain.

Eating right doesn't just mean ordering from the healthy food options when you go out to eat. In fact, the best way to eat properly is to make sure you know what to look for before you even enter the supermarket. Because the best foods you can eat are most likely the ones you prepare in your own kitchen.

That's why it's essential to make sure you have certain foods always available. You and your family will thank you in the long run:

1. **Kale** — Contains cancer-fighting antioxidants, promotes eye and skin health, and may strengthen the immune system.

2. **Sardines** — One of the best sources of mood boosting omega-3 fats, they don't contain as many chemicals as other larger fish.

3. **Pomegranate** — High in antioxidants, they help eliminate harmful free radicals, which may contribute to a variety of harmful conditions like heart disease, Alzheimer's, and cancer.

4. **Oatmeal** — Eating a bowl of oatmeal will not only help you reduce your LDL "bad" cholesterol, but it could also help you lose weight if you eat it before exercising.

5. **Quinoa** — Very similar to rice, this whole grain is packed with fiber and protein.

6. **Kefir** — Don't let the strange name fool you. This "yogurt in a glass" is full of beneficial probiotics that give your immune system a little extra boost.

7. **Lentils** — Another rice substitute, this wonder grain contains high amounts of both protein and fiber. Not to mention it's loaded with iron and folate. Lentils are extremely versatile and can be added to many recipes.

HOW TO AVOID SEEING YOUR DOCTOR

Remember the old saying, "An apple a day keeps the doctor away." Your mother or pediatrician probably told you that when you were younger to make sure you were eating your fruits and vegetables. Now that you're a bit older, you probably need to do more than eat properly to stay healthy. But the one thing that doctors will still tell you is that the best way to avoid seeing them is early prevention.

We've covered many ways to prevent certain ailments, but there are three big ones that threaten the lives of millions of Americans: heart disease, cancer, and diabetes.

If you want your car to run for a long time, you need to make sure the things you put into it (like gas and oil) don't end up ruining it. The same goes with your body. The food/fuel you consume either promotes or destroys your body's natural systems. Stop consuming processed food and you'll reduce your risk for heart disease, cancer, and diabetes.

Losing weight is another simple remedy that reduces the risk of all three health dangers. Carrying around less weight reduces the workload of your heart. And maintaining a healthy weight ensures that you don't expose yourself to the onset of Type 2 diabetes, assuming you eat healthy. In fact, studies are coming out saying that being overweight or obese is clearly linked to specific types of cancer.

And finally, if you haven't already, you should really consider quitting smoking. It adds additional strain to the heart, raises blood sugar levels for diabetics, and increases the risk of lung cancer.

THE BEST WAYS TO LOSE WEIGHT AND STAY HEALTHY

One of the best ways to maintain a healthy lifestyle doesn't require you to take a daily supplement or become a vegetarian. In fact, the only real requirement is that you have a more active role in how you live your life. Make it a responsibility to understand the types of foods you put into your body, and take it upon yourself to exercise and stay active.

With that in mind, let's list some secrets you can take advantage of to help you lose weight and avoid common health problems:

1. **Portion Control** — Trusting yourself to not overeat is a difficult thing to do. It's so easy to go back for another serving of food that you can easily find yourself cheating at any diet you put yourself on. That's why it's important to set up concrete barriers to prevent you from cheating. One of the easier ways to do this is to serve your food on smaller plates. Even if you do go back for seconds, you won't be able to fill your plate with as much food. If smaller plates aren't an option, try to overload on healthy vegetables.

2. **Ditch "Low-Fat" Labels** — Many foods claiming to be low-fat sacrifice many healthy nutrients in the process. Also, to replace the fat content of many of these foods,

chemicals and other substances are added. In the end, the healthy alternative is anything but.

3. **Start Your Metabolism Early** — Your metabolism is the fat-burning processing center of your body. And making sure it starts as early as possible ensures that you're burning fat longer throughout the day. There's a reason why your parents told you that breakfast was the most important meal of the day. It jump-starts your system after hours of slumber and gets the body ready to create the energy it needs to function. Maintaining that metabolism throughout the day by eating small, healthy portions of food will ensure you're burning calories until you lay down to sleep again.

4. **Say Goodbye to Artificial Sweeteners** — Countless studies have debunked the idea that these artificial sweeteners are a healthy alternative to sugars. Instead of consumer sweeteners (or actual sugar), why not try naturally sweet foods, like fresh fruits. They're like nature's candy.

5. **Water Is Your Best Friend** — One of the easiest ways to eliminate unnecessary sugar and artificial sweeteners from your diet it to always drink water. It helps cleanse the body and will make it easier to lose those extra pounds.

6. **Fiber and Greens Are Your Friends** — Filling your body up with greens and vegetables high in dietary fiber will make your metabolism work harder and curb food cravings in the process.

7. **10,000 Steps a Day** — It's one small goal that could pay off big in the long run. It sounds like a huge number, but it doesn't have to be if you make small changes in your daily routine. Instead of having food delivered, go out and pick it up. Take the stairs instead of the elevator at least once a day. Invest in a cheap pedometer to keep track and you'll soon discover yourself surpassing your goal easily.

We live in a time where potable water is available practically everywhere in America. But just because the government says the water coming out of your sink is clean doesn't mean that you should drink it. Not without treating it first.

There are many water filters on the market today that allow you to take an extra preventative measure to ensure that the water you drink is free from harmful elements. What makes ZeroWater filters different is that they don't base their effectiveness on some arbitrary amount of time. Their filters don't "expire" after two months of use. Instead, they measure how clean the water is after it passes through its filter. Once it rises above a certain level, they recommend that you replace the filter.

So you don't have to worry about it expiring if you don't use it for a few months. Instead of stockpiling water, which takes up a large amount of space, these filters offer a cost- and space-effective way to provide you and your family with clean drinking water.

9 BUSINESS WITHOUT GOVERNMENT'S PERMISSION

Washington's desire to be a part of everyone's life extends far beyond what you do in your own home. In fact, some of the largest interventions happen at your place of work. Government's liberal interpretation of the Constitution's Commerce Clause has given them an easy way to make sure everyone is playing nice in the workplace. But instead of creating an environment that promotes success and generates growth, they place onerous regulations that stifle innovation and hinder productivity.

Thankfully, there are ways around these government-imposed obstacles. Ways to build a business and a career without having to get Uncle Sam's stamp of approval every step of the way. All that's required is that you keep an open mind to new possibilities.

Let's take a look at a workplace that doesn't require a government nanny to make sure things function properly.

WORKING WITHOUT UNCLE SAM LOOKING OVER YOUR SHOULDER

One of the best things about America is the freedom to come up with an idea and start a business around it. It's part of the American spirit that drove economic growth in this country for many years. In recent times, however, government's insistence that everyone follow arbitrary rules and regulations created by special interests impedes a once defining trait of American business.

Fortunately, there are some businesses that allow you to operate in relative freedom. Professions that don't require you to constantly fill out government forms every step of the way to make sure everything is up to code.

If you have a passion for writing and feel you have the ability to move someone to act with your ability to write, then copywriting might be the profession for you. Writing promotional or advertorial material for products is a rewarding career with tremendous upside if done successfully. But most importantly, you can do it without constant government intervention.

You won't have to buy and register special equipment. Nor will you have to make sure that what you write is permitted by the government. It's a job that has tremendous upside, allows you to create your own hours, and gives you the ability to work remotely.

If you think copywriting might not be the best option for you, but still have a passion for writing, then think about writing an e-book. With new technology making digital books more popular than ever, e-books are an exciting way to get your ideas out to readers all over the world. Current writers don't have to risk thousands of dollars getting their book produced in a physical form. And distribution is fast and painless if done properly.

But if working online isn't for you, there are still plenty of other business opportunities that are available to you. If the market conditions are right, money can be made by starting something as simple as a land-scaping business or painting service. Anything that requires you to have a face-to-face relationship with clients could potentially generate easy revenue. Best of all, you won't have to compete with other major brick-and-mortar competitors, like Wal-Mart and Target.

One thing you need to know as the scourge known as the Affordable Care Act (aka Obamacare) descends upon America is how to protect any business from many of its burdensome regulations. In an effort to appeal to small businesses, the writers of the massive piece of legislation wrote in several loopholes that exempt businesses from new regulations.

If you're thinking of starting a new business, do your best to keep the number of employees you hire under 50. That includes both full-time and part-time employees. The new regulations utilize an equation that takes into account both types of workers when determining whether you need to provide everyone with health insurance. If you're over the legal limit and don't provide insurance, you could wind up paying thousands of dollars in fines.

OUTSOURCING YOUR PROBLEMS

Once you've started a business, you're bound to come across problems you never considered. They might be things as simple as accurately reporting inventory, or as complex as a problem regarding a computer program that's essential to your business' success. You could hire a consultant or contract an outside firm to take care of your problem. Or you could turn to one of America's growing alternatives to problem solving.

The next time you run into a dilemma, try outsourcing your problem to online communities who specialize in that field. Chris Anderson, American author and entrepreneur, ran into several problems in the early stages of his DIY Drones business. Instead of hiring an expert to get things right, he posted the problems he had to various online forums.

Obviously, there is risk in doing this. You expose your potentially groundbreaking idea to the general public, who may or may not try to claim it as their own. But if you're careful not to reveal too much information, you should be fine. And the information you receive back from these online experts could save you thousands of dollars in the early stages.

HOW TO NEGOTIATE WITH THE BEST OF THEM

One of the most essential skills to have when dealing with other people, both professionally and personally, is how to negotiate if the need should arise. Making sure you get what you need and don't get swindled in the process is essential. At the same time, however, you don't want to ruin your relationship with a potential business partner.

One simple negotiating trick requires a little planning and the resolve to stick with your guns. Before going into any meeting, make sure you decide on a range of prices or deals you're willing to accept. It's important that you make yourself flexible and not dead set on one fixed solution.

When negotiations start, be blunt and honest, and ask them what they're willing to offer. If their offer is within the range you've set in your head, you can agree, shake hands, and part ways knowing you are better off. If the offer is outside your predetermined range, simply decline politely and tell them that it's too much.

If they come back and offer a better deal, one that's within your range, that's great. But by avoiding the back and forth that's typical of the negotiation practice, you avoid risking a future successful relationship over potentially small compromises.

DON'T PUT ALL YOUR EGGS IN ONE BASKET

Starting a successful business is great, and it could provide you with a comfortable life/retirement. But relying on only one stream of income could be dangerous if something unexpected happens later on down the road. To ensure that your stream of income and your way of life remain safe, think about investing in multiple businesses.

Doing so will protect you from market swings that might affect only one or two parts of the economy. You'll rest easy knowing that you have other income sources if one or two fail.

It will be hard work, for sure. Being successful, especially without Uncle Sam's help, doesn't come easy. But it's this type of hard work that has proven time and time again to be the key factor in what makes a person successful. It's the extra time and effort you put into getting the right message across to your customers that makes them decide to buy from you, instead of their competitors.